CERAMICS FOR BEGINNERS

wheel throwing

Emily Reason

LARK
CRAFTS

A Division of Sterling Publishing Co., Inc.

New York / London

SENIOR EDITOR: Suzanne J. E. Tourtillott

EDITOR: Chris Rich

ART DIRECTOR: Kathleen Holmes

ART PRODUCTION: Carol Morse

ILLUSTRATOR: Orrin Lundgren

PHOTOGRAPHER: Lynne Harty

COVER DESIGNER: Celia Naranjo

Library of Congress Cataloging-in-Publication Data

Reason, Emily.
  Ceramics for beginners. Wheel throwing / Emily Reason.
     p. cm.
  Includes index.
  ISBN 978-1-60059-244-7 (hc-plc with jacket : alk. paper)
  1. Pottery craft. I. Title. II. Title: Wheel throwing.
  TT920.R43 2009
  738.1'4--dc22
                                  2009014893

10 9 8 7 6 5 4 3 2

Published by Lark Books, A Division of
Sterling Publishing Co., Inc.
387 Park Avenue South, New York, NY 10016

Text © 2010, Emily Reason
Photography © 2010, Lark Books, a Division of Sterling Publishing Co., Inc.,
unless otherwise specified
Illustrations © 2010, Lark Books, a Division of Sterling Publishing Co., Inc.,
unless otherwise specified

Distributed in Canada by Sterling Publishing,
c/o Canadian Manda Group, 165 Dufferin Street
Toronto, Ontario, Canada M6K 3H6

Distributed in the United Kingdom by GMC Distribution Services,
Castle Place, 166 High Street, Lewes, East Sussex, England BN7 1XU

Distributed in Australia by Capricorn Link (Australia) Pty Ltd.,
P.O. Box 704, Windsor, NSW 2756 Australia

If you have questions or comments about this book, please contact:
Lark Books, 67 Broadway, Asheville, NC 28801
828-253-0467

Manufactured in China

ISBN 13: 978-1-60059-244-7

For information about custom editions, special sales, premium and corporate
purchases, please contact Sterling Special Sales Department at 800-805-5489
or specialsales@sterlingpub.com.

For information about desk and examination copies available to college and
university professors, requests must be submitted to academic@larkbooks.com.
Our complete policy can be found at www.larkbooks.com.

contents

Introduction

The first time I witnessed a pot being thrown, I was immediately enthralled with the slow, rhythmic rotation of the wheel and the seemingly effortless motion of the potter's hands. Watching a soft, shiny lump of clay being transformed into a large, bulbous vase was hypnotic then and still hasn't ceased to captivate me.

INITIALLY, I LOVED CLAY SIMPLY FOR HOW IT FELT— FOR ITS SMOOTHNESS MASSAGING MY PALMS AS THE WHEEL SPUN. Later, I learned that I'm fascinated by all the ways in which a pot develops as it's made, refined, and fired. Clay is a large part of my life now; I love to share the joy of working with it.

Much like a beginning pottery class, *Wheel Throwing* is designed to offer a step-by-step, hands-on introduction to the basic techniques that every successful wheel thrower has learned. I've presented the information within these pages in a specific sequence that's designed to build your skills by adding new ones gradually, so I strongly recommend that you read the sections in the order of their appearance.

You'll start by learning about clay itself: how to select and store it, how to prepare it for throwing, and how to identify the changes that clay goes through as it dries. Next, you'll find out how to set up a safe and efficient workspace, and how to begin collecting your clay-working tools and supplies. You'll also be introduced to the concept of "form"—the volume and shape of a pot, and the visual relationship among its different parts.

Then comes the hands-on part. First, you'll learn how to center a lump of clay on the wheel, throw a basic cylinder form, and make a handle. Then you'll practice these techniques by creating three beautiful ceramic pieces of your own: a mug, a pitcher, and a fluted baking dish. All three projects are based on the cylinder form, and all of them are great examples of how variations on a single, basic wheel-throwing technique can produce very different results. Because the projects in *Wheel Throwing* are 100 percent functional, each time you make one, you'll experience the satisfaction that comes from being able to use what your hands have created.

After you've mastered the cylinder, you'll move on to the second basic form from which all wheel-thrown vessels are derived—the bowl. You'll also learn how to trim a "foot" (the clay base that a bowl form stands on). Then, once again, you'll put these new skills to use by making projects that showcase them: an elegant plate and lovely berry bowl. As you read on, you'll add more complex techniques to your repertoire, including how to decorate clay surfaces and how to throw lids and spouts. The culminating projects, a teapot and tulipiere, will give you a chance to bring together everything that you've learned, and the overviews of glazing and firing that follow will allow you to finish the surface of each pot you've thrown.

Every project in this book comes with a list of the special tools you'll need to make it, easy-to-follow instructions, a handy Related Techniques section that points you to pages you may want to re-read as refreshers, and how-to photographs that show you exactly what to do. At the end of each one is a description of the surface treatment that I used, in case you'd like to try for a similar effect. To provide you with some inspiration along the way, you'll find photographic galleries of wheel-thrown works by some of today's finest ceramists.

Wheel throwing takes a good bit of practice to master, of course, but if you're patient and persevere at a pace that's comfortable for you, you'll succeed. I encourage you to make multiples of every piece; throwing them will not only serve as good practice, but will also allow you to explore the possibilities offered by treating similar pots in slightly different ways. In time, you'll be able to combine different forming and surface techniques to create an almost infinite number of variations. And after you become accomplished at the wheel, if you'd like to try clay work without one, take a look at Shay Amber's *Hand Building*, the first book in Lark's *Ceramics for Beginners* series. A basic knowledge of both hand building and wheel forming can only enhance your work.

Handmade pottery represents the best of two worlds to me—both the visual and the functional. The dishes I've made sit on an exposed shelf so that I can luxuriate in the enjoyment of looking at them and grab them whenever I need to use them. The process of wheel throwing enriches my life, while the products enrich the appearance of my home and the food that I serve in it. I hope that as you read this book, you'll roll up your sleeves, get dirty, and find your own love of wheel throwing.

From Clay to Ceramic

Clay is a fascinating material. A lump of this soft, malleable stuff, formed with your own hands on a spinning potter's wheel, can become a useful and durable object of virtually any size or shape. Through the rewarding process of throwing clay, you'll craft this very basic material into something beautiful and functional, then add fire to make it a complete piece of art.

Ceramics suppliers sell ready-to-use clay in bagged, moist blocks.

■ THE CERAMIC PROCESS

Bringing a dried clay object to a high temperature until it becomes an unalterably changed ceramic piece is called *firing*. The heat required for this amazing transformation is attained in a special oven called a *kiln*. During the firing process, you control the kiln's rate of temperature change as well as the maximum temperature it reaches. Most clays are roughly classified according to the firing temperature required to cause the clay to *vitrify*. Vitrification is the tightening, hardening, and partial glassification of heated clay. Fully vitrified clay has been fired to *maturity*—the point at which the clay particles are most compressed; at this stage, the clay has been permanently changed into ceramic material.

■ CLAY BODIES AND GROG

The clay that you use for throwing starts as an organic material that's dug from the earth; it consists of fine particles of eroded rock. You might find a vein of sticky clay in the banks of a nearby stream, but it would be filled with rocks, sticks, and various mineral impurities, and would take a lot of sweat to make suitable for ceramic work. A more reliable source is your local ceramics supplier, who carries many types of clay, each of which has been mixed from dried and purified organic materials. It's best to start with one type of clay and come to know it well by using it. Experimentation, as you'll soon discover, is a big part of the ceramic process.

CLAY BODIES are mixtures of clays, fluxes, and fillers. Earthenware and stoneware occur as raw clays but are blended, as is porcelain, into clay bodies to make them workable. Each one occupies a different section of the ceramic firing-range spectrum, and each has its own working properties, firing needs, and aesthetic qualities. I recommend working with either an earthenware or stoneware clay body; both stand up well to the rigors of being worked on the wheel. Before you purchase your clay, find out its maximum firing range, and make sure your kiln can attain the top recommended temperature necessary to fire the clay to maturity.

EARTHENWARE CLAY BODIES are red or white. The red version gets its color from the iron in it; the white lacks iron. Earthenware is a *low-fire* clay; it matures at around 1830°F (999°C). Because it doesn't shrink or warp much as it dries, it's good for both wheel throwing and hand building. It's usually less expensive to buy and fire

Left to right: Glaze-fired, bisque-fired, and unfired earthenware

than stoneware, too, which makes it appealing to use as you're learning.

STONEWARE CLAY BODIES vary greatly in color, from off-white and gray to dark brown. Brown stoneware, which has iron in it, fires with speckles on its surface. White stoneware contains less iron. Stoneware is typically a *high-fire* clay and

fires at much higher temperatures—2345°F (1285°C)—than earthenware, resulting in a very dense and nonporous ceramic material that's able to hold water. It's pleasant to throw, and its durability makes it ideal for *functional ware* (utilitarian objects such as dinnerware). Some stoneware bodies can be fired at slightly lower *mid-range* temperatures, around 2262°F (1239°C).

PORCELAIN is a pure white, dense, and durable clay that is free of iron. Like stoneware, it's a high-fire body, maturing around 2345°F (1285°C). A soft clay, it's rather difficult to throw, and is susceptible to cracking and warping during drying and firing. Porcelain is a beautiful clay body, but because it's tricky to work with and much more expensive than other clays, I don't recommend it for beginners.

Left to right: Glaze-fired, bisque-fired, and unfired stoneware

Grog is visible in the clay on the left; the clay on the right contains none.

GROG is a filler in a clay body; it's made from pulverized, fired clay. The sifted product, available in different particle sizes, from very fine to coarse, is sold according to the mesh size used to produce it. Fine grog, added to earthenware and stoneware clay for *tooth* (or roughness), gives the clay the ability to stand up to being worked, but it won't irritate your hands, as a coarser grog would. Most commercially prepared, moist clay bodies already have grog mixed into them.

■ STAGES OF DRYNESS

The process of making a wheel-thrown ceramic piece entails several basic steps: throwing the clay, letting it dry, firing it (a process known as *bisque firing*), glazing it, and firing it again in what's called a *glaze firing*. You can continue to modify or decorate a basic thrown form as it dries. Learning how to identify the stages of dryness and how to control them is important, since the level of moisture in the clay both permits and limits what you can do to your pots. Clay shrinks throughout the drying process as water evaporates from it, and pottery shrinks further during the firing, as the clay particles condense and flux together.

Clay at the *plastic stage* is wet—that is, moist and malleable. Generally, clay at this stage is also tacky; if you touch it, you'll leave fingerprints. All basic forming is done with plastic clay. (One note here: "Wet" doesn't mean dripping with water that you've added to it; it's the moist stage of a pot just after it's been shaped.) Bagged clay is sold in the plastic state. In order to keep fresh clay in the near-perfect moist state that it's in when you buy it, store it in its original bag, a heavy plastic bag, or a large, airtight container. Keep plastic bags sealed tightly, and position their sealed ends so that the weight of the clay is right on top of them. Use plastic sheeting to cover any clay that you've worked and plan to work with some more so that it will retain its moisture and remain pliable. Keep your clay away from heat and from freezing temperatures. If you use more than one clay body, separate and label each one, and take care not to inadvertently mix bits of one body with another.

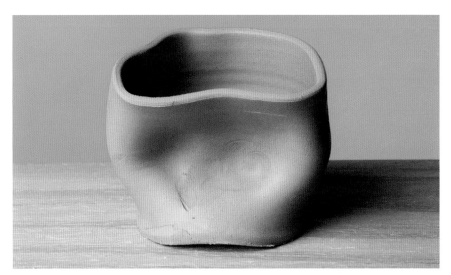

Clay that's just been thrown is wet and malleable, and will retain fingerprints when it's touched.

Leather-hard clay, which will give and crack under pressure, is soft enough to retain a fingernail impression, but hard enough not to show fingerprints.

Bone-dry clay won't accept a fingernail impression easily. It's brittle and will crack or break under pressure, so handle it gently.

▶ **Tip:** Clay that is drying and hasn't been fired yet is referred to as "green," and unfired ware is called "greenware."

As clay dries, it moves through the *leather-hard* stage, during which it ranges from soft to hard. Leather-hard clay is cool and somewhat dry, and feels much like leather to the touch. While it's still soft, it gives way to applied pressure. Once it's hard, forceful pressure will cause it to crack and touching it won't leave fingerprints, although pressing a fingernail into it will leave a mark. At the leather-hard stage, the clay is stiff enough to be handled without easily distorting its shape, so this is the time for trimming, carving, or otherwise altering a pot, or attaching a handle or spout.

When all of the physical water has evaporated from the clay, it's at the *bone-dry* stage and is ready for firing. (If a pot feels cool when you touch it to your cheek, it isn't bone dry yet; there's still moisture in it.) The lack of moisture in bone-dry clay lightens its color. No further shaping or attaching can be done once this stage of dryness has been reached, but you can use a plastic scouring pad to sand away any unwanted marks. Do this outdoors, and wear a respirator; free-floating clay dust is harmful to lungs.

The final stage of the drying process is bisque firing, which produces a permanent change in the clay. Clay should be bone dry before this firing takes place. If a still-wet pot were fired, the intense heat would create steam as it rapidly expelled the moisture in the clay, and the steam, in turn, could cause the clay to crack or even explode. Typically, bisque firing is done slowly in order to reduce the risk of damaging your lovely pots. The surface of bisque ware is hard and porous, and is wonderfully receptive to wet *glazes* (the materials that are fired onto pottery to create sealed, glassy surfaces).

A bisque-fired cup

When you're wedging, apply just enough pressure to make an impression in the clay; try not to press so hard that you smear it.

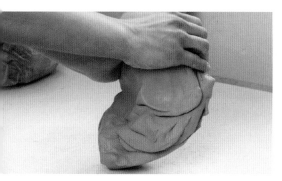

Rotating the clay helps to ensure that you wedge it throughout.

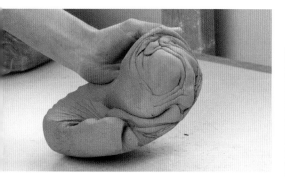

Wedging correctly creates a spiral in the clay.

▶ **Tip:** Before you wedge clay, consider using a kitchen scale to weigh the amount you intend to use for your project. Weighing is especially helpful when you want to make pieces that are similar in size.

■ WEDGING CLAY

Brand-new clay, as well as reclaimed clay (see the next section) must be prepared for throwing by *wedging* it. This process mixes the clay to the same consistency throughout, frees it of lumps, makes it easier to throw by loosening it, and also removes unwanted air pockets from clay that's already been worked. Do your wedging on a plaster, wood, or canvas surface so the clay won't stick, and make sure your wedging table is heavy, sturdy, and waist high.

To begin wedging, place the clay on the table and grasp it with both hands. Using the heels of your palms, press it down and away from you. Then rock the clay up and towards you while rotating it slightly. Repeat these steps, pressing the clay down and away, then rocking it upward and back toward you as you rotate it. Be careful not to fold the clay over onto itself; you don't want to trap air pockets in it. If this happens without your intending it to, you may be applying too much pressure.

Repeat the pressing-rocking-rotating process a few dozen times; your motions will become faster and more rhythmic. As you work, you'll see a spiral start to form at one end of the clay. Wedging may seem awkward at first, but you'll improve with practice. You'll know that you've wedged properly when the clay feels consistently smooth and is free of air pockets. When you've finished, smack the clay into a cone shape.

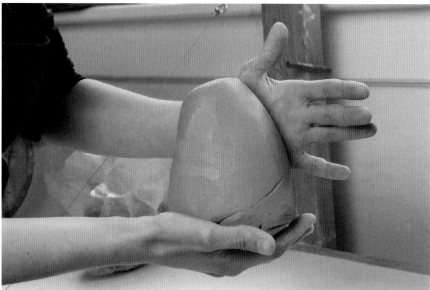

Throwing begins with a cone-shaped piece of well-wedged clay.

■ RECLAIMING CLAY

Scraps of clay can be reclaimed at any stage of dryness before firing. Collect them in a bucket, and add water to make a *slurry* (a wet, sloppy mixture). When you have a bucketful, spread the slurry out on a plaster slab; the plaster will absorb the excess water so that the clay becomes dry enough to wedge and use again. To make your own plaster slab, build a wooden frame, squish skinny coils of clay into the seams to seal them, and pour wet pottery plaster into the frame. Alternatively, you can purchase plaster bats or molds. Should you choose to mix up the plaster yourself, do it outdoors—even small bits of plaster in clay will ruin it.

Clay that's become too soft from throwing—making it difficult to work with—can also be reclaimed. To return it to a workable consistency, first form it into a rough coil shape, about 3 inches (7.6 cm) in diameter. Bend the coil into an arch, and press its ends onto the worktable. Air circulating around the coil will remove the excess moisture. Before using this clay again, be sure to wedge it.

To recycle unfired clay scraps, make a slurry, spread it out on a piece of plaster, and after the plaster has absorbed some of the moisture, peel up the clay and wedge it well.

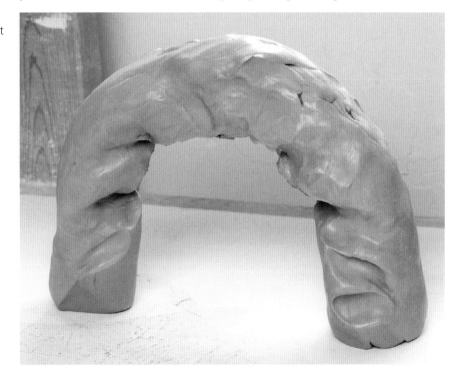

Shape clay that's become too soft into an arch, and let it dry out a bit in the open air.

The Studio Setting

A good clay studio is simply a place that's comfortable, safe to work in, and located in an area apart from your living space. A basement, garage, or shed makes a great work space if it's properly heated. You'll need a floor that's easy to mop, good lighting, and running water, too. Furnish your studio with a solid worktable and some shelves; secondhand or homemade items of furniture work well.

Variable-speed potter's wheel and stool

POTTERY REQUIRES A GOOD BIT OF EQUIPMENT, BUT YOU DON'T NEED MUCH TO GET STARTED. This chapter covers only what's required to make the projects in this book. Start by investing in the necessities, and acquire other items when you're ready.

■ THE POTTER'S WHEEL

THE POTTER'S WHEEL is your most important tool, of course. Its rotating wheel head provides the working surface and the motion required to make thrown pottery. A *variable-speed wheel* has a foot pedal, and although it tends to be more expensive than a *kick wheel*, which is powered by kicking a flywheel at your feet, it's good to learn on. The proper direction of the wheel is counterclockwise. Some wheels allow you to reverse this rotation, which lefties may find handy, but because not all wheels have a reverse option, I recommend learning to throw with a counterclockwise spin. (The instructions in this book are based on the wheel spinning in this direction.)

You'll also need a **STOOL** when you're at the wheel—one tall enough to allow your legs to create a 90° angle when you're seated.

▦ THE ESSENTIAL TOOL KIT

Each project in this book comes with a list of any special tools and equipment that you'll need to make it, but this list *doesn't* include the common items that every potter has on hand. No matter what kind of piece you're throwing, keep the following tools with you at the wheel; you'll need them for almost every piece you throw.

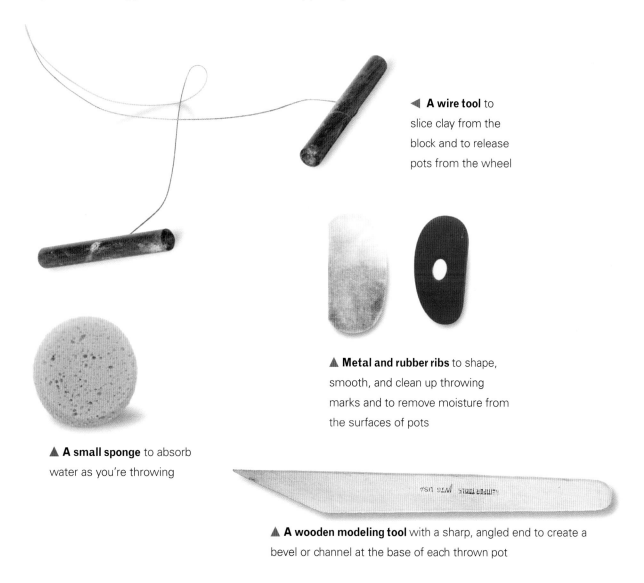

◀ **A wire tool** to slice clay from the block and to release pots from the wheel

▲ **Metal and rubber ribs** to shape, smooth, and clean up throwing marks and to remove moisture from the surfaces of pots

▲ **A small sponge** to absorb water as you're throwing

▲ **A wooden modeling tool** with a sharp, angled end to create a bevel or channel at the base of each thrown pot

▲ **A needle tool** to level uneven rims of pots, as well as to cut through clay

■ COMMON TOOLS OF THE TRADE

The tools and equipment described in this section are also important, although you don't have to keep them right next to your wheel and you won't need every one of them right away. They're *not* included in the special tools list that's provided with each project, but many of the projects do require them, so make sure you read the project instructions before you begin.

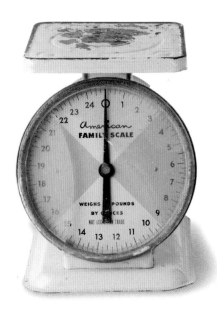

▲ **A kitchen scale** is useful for weighing out equal amounts of clay when you want to throw pots of similar sizes for a set or series.

▲ **Plastic containers with lids**, ranging in size from 1 pint (.5 L) to 5 gallons (19 L) are useful for holding throwing water and for storing *slip* (a liquid form of clay), glaze, and clay scraps. Yogurt containers and restaurant castoffs, washed free of oil, are fine.

▲ **A small chamois** smooths the rims of pots nicely.

▲ **Ware boards**, which are used to transport and store thrown pots, can be made of wood or of drywall that's at least ½ inch (1.3 cm) thick. Cover the exposed plaster edges of drywall with duct tape.

▶ **Plastic sheeting** draped over thrown pots and wedged clay that's waiting to be thrown keeps clay from drying out too much and too quickly. Plastic drop cloths and dry-cleaning bags work well, too.

▲ **A spray bottle** filled with water allows you to mist your pots in order to keep them moist when you want to do further work on them.

▲ **Large sponges** are good for general studio cleaning tasks.

▶ **Bats** are round, removable disks that fit onto wheel heads. Potters use them to throw large and flat forms. They provide a surface area for throwing and allow you to remove your thrown pots without having to grasp and possibly distort them. The best bats are made of plaster or dense fiberboard, but plastic ones also work. **Bat pins**, which are similar to bolts with wing nuts, fit through holes on the wheel head to hold the bats in place.

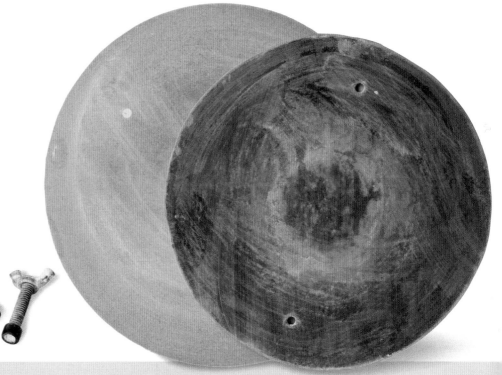

◀ **A foam-covered bat** helps to keep large forms stable on the wheel for trimming. For instructions on how to make one, see page 119.

■ SPECIAL TOOLS AND SUPPLIES

As your skills improve and you tackle more challenging projects, your tool collection will begin to grow. Purchase the tools and other items described in this section on an as-needed basis. Because you may not own any of them yet, when they're required to make a project in this book, they're listed with that project.

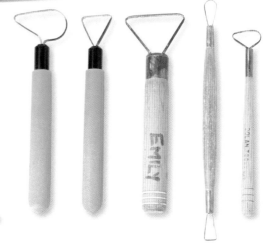

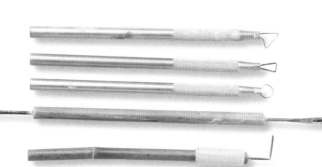

▲ **Carving tools** are used to incise decorative designs into clay surfaces.

▲ **Trimming tools** are used to make *foot rings* (the ring-like feet at the bottoms of pots) and to remove excess clay in other areas. Some can also be used for carving. **Ribbon tools**—trimming tools with looped, sharp-edged wires at one end—are useful for cutting into clay and come in flat or round shapes that define the profiles they create on pots.

▲ **Wooden modeling tools** in a variety of shapes are useful for cutting and blending clay, and for making impressions in it.

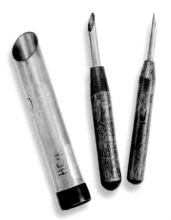

◀ **Hole-making tools** are helpful for creating spout holes in clay teapots, as well as the holes in clay colanders and planters.

▶ **Pencils and chopsticks** work well for carving and signing pots, and for making guide marks on clay.

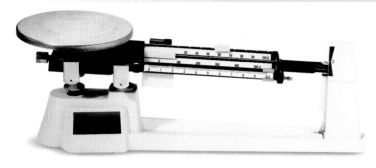

▲ **A metric scale** is required when you want to weigh the dry materials for a hand-mixed batch of slip or glaze.

▲ **Scoring tools and serrated ribs** have teeth that are used to roughen clay surfaces on pieces that you want to attach to each other.

▼ **Knives**, both short and long, are good for cutting clay to make handles, spouts, and slabs. A small knife with a double-edged blade is useful for many of the projects in this book.

▶ **Ceramic chucks** hold pots that won't stand on their own when they're turned upside down. Once you learn how to throw, making your own chucks is easy (see page 119).

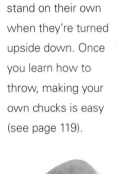

◀ **A wooden rib** is used to shape thrown forms.

▲ **Calipers** are measuring tools that you'll use to gauge the diameter of a pot's rim when you want to make a lid for it.

◀ **Brushes,** both natural bristle and foam, are used to apply slip, wax, underglaze, and/or glaze. You can practice your brushwork with India ink on newsprint.

▼ A rolling pin is handy for making flat clay slabs.

◀ **A piece of foam**, with its soft surface, can serve as a base on which to set an inverted pot to dry. Half-inch-thick (1.3 cm) foam is available at many fabric stores.

▲ **A banding wheel,** which is essentially a turntable, elevates a pot to a comfortable height when you want to decorate it, and allows you to rotate the pot so that you can see all of its sides.

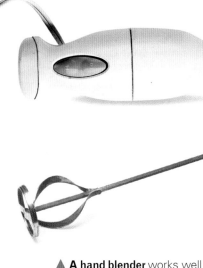

▲ **A hand blender** works well for mixing small amounts of slip or glaze to a smooth consistency. For larger amounts, an electric drill and paint-mixing attachment work better.

▲ **Slip trailers** (slip-trailing bulbs, hair-dye bottles, ketchup bottles, syringes, and baby nasal aspirators) are squeezable slip applicators that are used to create textured slip decorations.

◀ **A sieve** is necessary when you make glaze and slip from scratch; you smooth the liquid mix by pouring it through one. Sieves are rated according to the size of the particulate matter you wish to trap; start with an 40-mesh one.

Make sure you wear a respirator whenever you sand or grind pottery, make clay or glaze from scratch, or do anything in your studio that creates potentially harmful dust.

Gloves are critical when you're working with dry glaze and slip ingredients.

To avoid creating a lot of dirty laundry, wear an apron and wash it frequently so that it doesn't store dust.

▓ SAFETY

Making pottery is a fun hobby—and can be perfectly safe if you observe standard precautions in your studio.

Dust is the biggest safety issue for potters, so whenever possible, perform all dust-creating tasks outdoors, and follow a regular studio-cleaning regimen. A clean studio is a healthy one. Wipe your work surfaces with a wet sponge, and keep the floor clear of clay scraps that might otherwise be trampled into fine dust. The best way to keep the floor clean is with a vacuum equipped with a HEPA filter, and with a mop. *Don't* dry-sweep; you'll just move the dust around.

Avoid plumbing issues by investing in a sink-trap system or by keeping a dishpan in your sink for initial rinsing of clay-covered tools. Clay can clog drains,

so don't pour the rinse water down the drain. Instead, let the clay that's in the dishpan settle to the bottom; then pour off the water and discard the settled clay. Collect all clay bits and place them in a scrap bucket.

Dress for success in the studio. Keep long hair tied back so that it won't get caught in the spinning wheel. Remove all jewelry and your watch, and keep your fingernails trimmed. Designate a pair of shoes to wear in the studio so that you don't track dust into your home. Wear a respirator or dust mask any time you sand or grind pottery, make clay or glaze from scratch, or do anything that creates dust. Protect your eyes with dark safety glasses when you look inside a hot kiln, and wear long

rubber gloves when you're mixing glaze from dry powders or handling a liquid glaze that contains potentially harmful ingredients.

Learn about the materials that you keep in your studio, especially glaze and slip ingredients, which can be hazardous to your health. Read their labels and the *MSDS* (Material Safety Data Sheet) information that manufacturers and distributors often provide. (MSDS information for many materials is also available online.) Read the warnings, and the instructions for proper handling and use. And remember: a respirator will only work if you wear it! Label all containers with bold, clear lettering, and make special note of any toxic elements.

Form: An Object and an Idea

As a beginner, your first concern will be with gaining control of the clay, but every potter must also gain an appreciation of the importance of form. In its widest sense, this term refers to all the visible aspects of a three-dimensional pot. To study form is to look at volume, shape, and how the various parts of a pot relate to one another. The form of a well-executed pot can resemble the movements of an accomplished dancer: graceful, fluid, and beautifully joined.

■ THE ELEMENTS OF A POT

The essential elements of a pot, all of which have an effect on its overall form, are named as if they were body parts (see figure 1). The *lip* (or rim) is the opening at the top of the pot, and the *foot* is its base. A shapely piece sometimes has a tapered *neck* that serves as the transition between the pot's *shoulder* and lip. A pot that is round is said to have a *belly* (or *hip*).

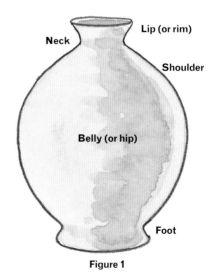

Lip (or rim)

Neck

Shoulder

Belly (or hip)

Foot

Figure 1

■ VOLUME AND PROPORTION

Volume and *proportion* both influence form. Volume is the space inside a pot and can be minimal, as it is in a small pot with vertical walls, or full, as it is when the belly of a pot is expanded. Volume affects both the physical and visual attributes of a form.

Proportional relationships exist among the many parts of a pot. Physically, your pot must have balanced proportions so that it won't topple over. Proportion also affects the ways in which the parts of a pot relate to create a visually balanced and pleasing form. The jar shown below provides a good example of full volume and balanced proportions.

■ INSPIRATION AND SKETCHING

There's no better source of inspiration than handmade pottery itself. Museums and books are great sources for historical pottery and images of it, and at shops and craft shows you can often handle contemporary pieces. Observe a piece from every angle; if possible, rotate it in your hands. Notice the subtle characteristics that give a handmade pot visual interest. Its *profile* (or outline) may flow in an interesting way, where a convex curve transitions smoothly into a concave one, for example. Look also for any parts that were given special treatment, such as a tall foot; a plump, well-defined rim; or an exaggerated spout on a tiny teapot. Take a look at the carafe shown in the middle below, and note the contrast between its long body and understated handle. Also notice how well its wide, round foot grounds the piece. The pitcher in the right below illustrates elegant proportions.

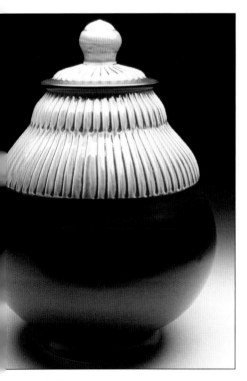

Emily Reason
Carved Jar, 2008

17 x 12 inches (43.2 x 30.5 cm)
Wheel-thrown porcelain; cone 10, reduction fired
Photo by Artist

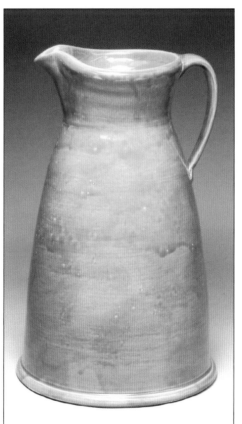

Jay Owens
Wine Carafe 3, 2005

16 x 9 x 8 inches (40.6 x 22.9 x 20.3 cm)
Wheel-thrown red earthenware; electric fired, cone 04; white slip, alkaline glaze, sgraffitto
Photo by Artist

Amy Evans
Untitled, 2004

12 x 5 x 5 inches (30.5 x 12.7 x 12.7 cm)
Wheel-thrown stoneware; soda fired, cone 9
Photo by Chuck McMahon and Artist

Keep your eyes open to the everyday forms that surround you, as well. Study landscape features such as rolling hills, architectural structures and rooflines, and the profiles of household items, and make quick sketches of them. Use descriptive words to describe their forms: "angular," "soft," "rigid," "full," "delicate," or "rugged," for example. Architecture can be a wonderful source of inspiration as you consider possible forms, as illustrated by the piece shown at the right. The top of the vase shown below was inspired by the dome of a cathedral.

Emily Reason
Carved Vase, 2008

5 x 5 x 8 inches (12.7 x 12.7 x 20.3 cm)
Cone 10, reduction fired
Photo by Artist

The Cathedral of Christ the Savior, Moscow
Photo by Carl Palka

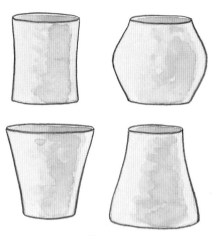

Figure 2

In your sketchbook, make quick drawings of pots that you think convey these adjectives, and additional drawings that show changes in volume and proportion. Sketching different profiles of the pot you'd like to throw can give you a sense of the dramatic possibilities that even small changes can make. As you can see in figure 2, a basic cylinder form can be varied greatly by increasing its volume or changing its proportions. The practice of looking closely and sketching will help you develop a sense of form, which is as much a part of the creation process as throwing itself.

■ THE TWO ESSENTIAL FORMS

The two most basic forms in wheel-thrown pottery are the cylinder and the bowl (see figures 3 and 4). As soon as you acquire the basic skills needed to throw them, you'll learn how cylinders and bowls can become cups, teapots, and dishes. A cylinder becomes a pitcher when it's given curves, a spout, and a handle. A bowl is transformed into a plate when it's widened and flattened. Every project in this book starts as one of these two forms, so you have some opportunities to practice ahead of you!

In the chapters that follow, you'll not only learn how to throw, but you'll also discover the characteristics that make cylinder and bowl forms so different from each other. Before making any projects, take the time to throw several cylinders. After that, throw several bowls. Treat these pieces as exercises rather than as finished works that you'll want to glaze, fire, and keep.

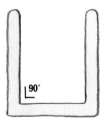

**Cross section
of a cylinder**

Figure 3

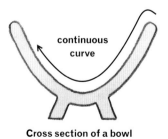

continuous
curve

Cross section of a bowl

Figure 4

Technique: **Centering**

Centering—making sure that the clay you plan to throw is centered on the wheel—is the very first thing you do at the potter's wheel. Although the technique can be quite challenging, it must be mastered. The process takes practice, awareness of your posture and the pressure you apply to the clay, and some hand-eye coordination.

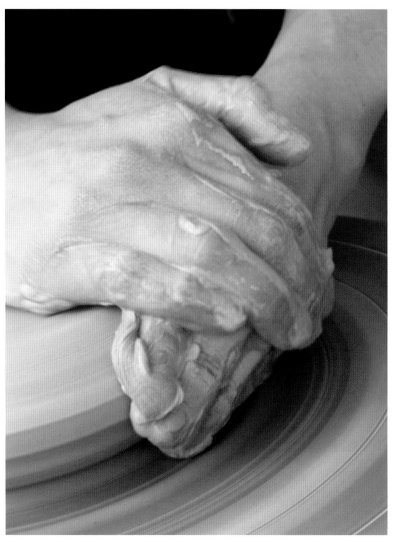

The centering process begins with throwing a 2-pound (.9 kg) ball of clay forcefully down onto the center of the *wheel head* (the metal disk on the wheel), using the concentric rings on the head as location guides. Using force will help the clay to stick. (Don't worry if the ball of clay is a little off center.) Once the clay is in place, don't touch it again unless the wheel is in motion.

To maintain the control you need to center properly, your arms, shoulders, and knees must be solidly braced. Anchor your elbows on your thighs, just above your knees, and lock your shoulders and elbows when touching the spinning clay. **1** A comfortable posture is essential when you're centering; you shouldn't feel tense or strained.

The next step is *coning* (raising the clay upward into a conical shape); it acts as an extension of wedging and also works some moisture into the clay. Start by setting the wheel spinning at medium speed. Do keep in mind that a variable-speed wheel, which is usually controlled by means of a foot pedal, can turn much faster than you would ever need or want. Never run the wheel at full speed; very high speeds make it too easy to lose control of the clay.

Wet your hands and grip the clay from the sides, overlapping your left hand over your right. To make the clay rise naturally into a conical shape, squeeze it by applying pressure with the areas between your fingertips and the heels of your palms, while simultaneously raising your hands upward. The clay will begin to rise into a cone. **2** As you approach the top, ease up on the pressure you apply.

One attempt at squeezing and lifting the clay in this manner is called a *pull*. One to two pulls should make a suitable cone. (At this stage, it's okay if the cone wobbles a little.) Your hand movements on the spinning clay should be consistent and about equal in speed to the speed of the wheel. For example, if your wheel speed is fast, you can use more pressure and make a faster pull. If the wheel speed is slow, make the pull slowly.

▶ **Tip:** Be aware of your posture while throwing. Position the wheel head so that it's level with your bellybutton, and keep your back straight as you lean over it. If necessary, place blocks of wood under the wheel legs in order to adjust the height.

Learning to throw is a little like learning to drive. At first, it may feel like too much to do all at the same time. There's the wheel in your hands, your foot on the gas, the lane markings…but with practice you'll learn how to maintain a steady wheel speed while you apply just the right amount of pressure to the clay.

If at any time you feel the clay dragging or tearing under your hands, just wet them again—but don't overdo it. Too much water saturates and weakens clay, so never use so much that it makes puddles on the wheel head. Simply dip your hands in water; you only need enough to allow your hands to glide over the clay. If the clay tears or detaches from the wheel head, you may be gripping it too tightly. **3** Start over with another piece of wedged clay, and ease up on the pressure you apply. A wheel head that's too wet may cause the clay to slip off center. **4** Dry off the head with a towel, and reposition the clay by hurling it back into place.

The last step of centering is working the clay back down close to the wheel head. Position your left palm against the clay at the nine o'clock position, so that the clay spins into it for maximum resistance. Rest the thumb of that hand across the top of the clay, place the heel of your right palm over it, and use the heel to press your thumb down onto the clay, keeping your arms at a 90° angle as you do. **5** You may have to lift your right elbow off your thigh for this step. At this point, most of the pressure you're applying is coming from your right hand; the left hand rests as it holds its position.

▶ **Tip:** Centering is more about judicious hand positioning, pressure, and bracing than about muscling the clay into place. Work *with* the spinning of the wheel and the weight of the clay, not against them.

As you press down on the spinning clay, it spreads out. When you've worked it down to the point at which the edge of your left palm makes contact with the wheel head, apply smooth pressure with the fingertips of your left hand—pressure that's equal to the pressure you're applying with your other hand. Continue to hold your arms steady and fixed at a 90° angle so your hands form a vise-like grip that forces the clay on center. **6**

Sit back from the wheel. If the clay spins without wobbling, you've been successful! If it's not quite centered, continue to compress the clay between both hands. If it wobbles more in one area—at one side, for example—exert more pressure there, gripping the clay with the fingertips of your left hand.

Technique: **Throwing a Cylinder**

The first form every potter learns to throw is the cylinder—a form that is slightly taller than it is wide, and about as wide at the rim as it is at the base. Its wall and base form an angle of about 90° (see figure 3 on page 25). Beginners often find that making bowls comes more easily than making cylinders because the centrifugal force of a quick-spinning wheel naturally pulls clay outward, resulting in an open form rather than a narrow one. But first you'll learn how to resist centrifugal force rather than submit to it!

▦ SINKING A HOLE IN THE CENTER

For your first several attempts, use small amounts of clay—about 1 pound (.45 kg) each time. After you've become more proficient, you can throw larger amounts. Weigh and wedge several pieces of clay in advance, and make sure that everything you need is within arm's reach of the wheel. **1**

Start by coning and centering a piece of clay. Next, while the wheel is spinning, sink a hole in the center of the clay. Rest two fingers atop the clay and, starting from the outer edge, move them toward the middle until you feel less friction under your fingertips. You've found the center. Now use the index and middle fingers of your right hand to make a hole by pressing straight down into the center. Be sure to watch how deep you go; don't poke through the bottom of the clay. **2**

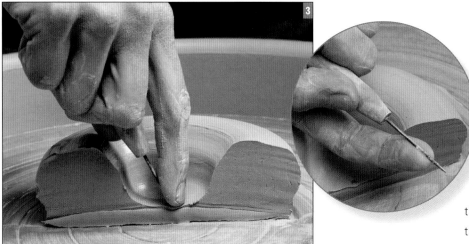

To check the thickness of the bottom, push a needle tool through the clay until it hits the wheel head. Place the fingernail of your index finger on the tool where it emerges from the clay. Then remove the needle, leaving your fingernail in place to mark the thickness. **3** That thickness should be relative to how thick you intend to make the walls of the pot, but a good general depth is ¼ inch (6 mm).

▨ EXPANDING THE HOLE

To open the hole wider, rest your left hand on the outside of the clay, place the curled index and middle fingers of your right hand inside the pot, at the six o'clock position, and pull your hands toward your body. **4** To avoid throwing the clay off center, use a slow-medium wheel speed, gradual hand motions, and moderate pressure. The interior bottom of the pot should be flat.

Next, you must *compress* the base. Think of compressing as the opposite of stretching. It serves two purposes: it eases the stress imposed on stretched clay particles and also keeps them aligned so the pot will be less prone to cracking. To compress clay, you apply inward pressure at the pot's rim, base, or elsewhere, using your fingers, a tool, or a combination of the two. To compress the base here, press your first three fingers lightly down on the bottom as you move them from the outer edge in to the center. **5** Repeat this motion a few times.

PULLING THE CYLINDER

Now it's time to give the pot some height by pulling the clay upward to make the walls taller and thinner. The first pull is the *power pull*—a slightly aggressive one, the purpose of which is to move a lot of clay at one time. The wheel speed for this step should be slow-medium. With the fingers of your left hand inside the pot and your thumb outside so that the clay spins away from its tip, hold the clay with a claw-like grip. Rest your right hand over your left. **6** Your right hand is mostly at rest in this case, but you should always approach the clay with both hands for good balance. Now rotate your left wrist slightly and apply pressure with your thumb at the base of the pot, pulling slightly upward and inward at the same time. During a power pull, your left hand does the work, while your right provides balance and stability. The fingers inside the pot should simply resist the pressure applied by your thumb. If the rim of the pot flares outward (a natural result of centrifugal force) or if you don't feel that you have good control, your wheel may be spinning too fast.

To proceed with regular pulls, first position your hands on the right side of the wheel, at about three to four o'clock, so the clay spins away from, not into, your fingertips. Place your left fingertips inside the pot, at the very bottom, and your right fingertips slightly lower, on the outside bottom. **7**

▶ **Tip:** If water accumulates on the inside of the pot at any time, remove it with a sponge while the wheel is in motion. Water left sitting in place will saturate the clay so that it sticks to the wheel when it's time to remove the finished piece.

To make vertical pulls, most of the pressure comes from the hand that's on the outside; the inside hand resists that pressure. Using a slow-medium wheel speed, begin the pull by pressing in at the base with your right hand, scooping the clay to draw it upward and slightly inward. **8** Repeat pulling two to four times until the desired height is established and the cylinder's walls are as thick at the base as they are at the rim. As you practice, your goal should be to make fewer yet more effective pulls.

Is your cylinder's rim uneven? **9** Take a look at Troubleshooting on page 34. To level the rim, first ease the tip of a needle tool gently through the clay, just underneath the lowest point on the rim. Then hold the needle tool in place as the wheel turns; it will trim off the excess clay and can be used to lift that clay away.

As you practice throwing cylinders, a good way to see how well you've distributed the clay throughout a thrown piece is to cut through each of your first few attempts with a wire tool and view the cross section. **10** The walls should be even in thickness. If they're not, refer to Troubleshooting on page 34.

▶ **Tip:** The throwing process should be relatively quick. When it isn't, the overworked clay gets weak and tired. After several attempts at centering or after dozens of pulls, clay becomes saturated and overstretched. If your clay becomes very soft, you're better off starting afresh. Form the clay into an arch, and let it dry out a little before reusing it (see page 13).

▓ FINISHING THE POT

To finish the exterior of your cylindrical pot, use a metal rib to smooth and clean it. Place your left hand inside the pot. Holding the rib in your right hand, place it against the pot, angling it away from you slightly, in the direction that the wheel is spinning, so the rib won't catch on the spinning clay. **11** To maintain control of the pot and the tool, be sure to hold the tool firmly and maintain your braced position. Now compress the walls lightly by pressing the clay between the tool and your left hand, beginning at the bottom and working upward. This process removes throwing marks as well as surface moisture. (A pot is easier to remove from the wheel when its surface is somewhat dry.)

Now, the moment of truth—taking your first cylinder off the wheel! Place a ware board nearby so you can transfer the pot to it easily while you're still seated, without any awkward reaching.

Hold a wooden modeling tool in your right hand like a pencil, and with the wheel spinning at medium speed, bring the tip of the tool to the base of the pot to cut a groove. **12** This groove will serve as a guide for your wire tool. Wrap the wire at each end of that tool around the fingers of each

hand, and pull the wire taut between your thumbs. The taut wire should be a couple of inches (5 cm) longer than the diameter of the base of your pot. Then hold the exposed wire flat against the wheel head, on the far side of the pot, and, while the wheel is spinning slowly, pull it toward you. **13**

Wipe your hands clean with a dry towel and cup them gently around the pot. Lifting up the front of the pot first, rotate it slightly to detach it from the wheel head, and transfer it to a ware board.

Allow the cylinder to dry for a little while, until its rim has stiffened. (The rim of a pot this size will stiffen in about 30 minutes.) Then flip it upside down so its base can dry to leather hard. Next, set the cylinder upright on a smooth surface, grasp it around the rim with one hand, tilt it, and smooth the edge of the base by rolling it on the work surface with a wrist-turning motion. 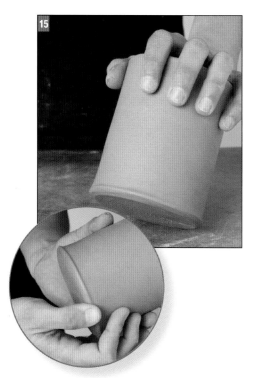 Now hold the cylinder up in one hand, and smooth the base further with the thumb of your other hand.

■ TROUBLESHOOTING

Throwing pots has its challenges. Following are descriptions of a few common ones and some remedies for the problems they can pose. Plenty of practice helps, of course!

Problem: One side of the rim is taller than the other.

Solution: An uneven rim is usually caused by pulling too fast when the wheel is spinning slowly. Be mindful of your hand and wheel speed, and try to coordinate them better. To trim an uneven rim, see the instructions on page 32.

Problem: The thickness of the cylinder walls isn't uniform on all sides.

Solution: The clay wasn't centered, or the hole you made in it wasn't directly in the middle. Take time to practice centering (see pages 26–28), and make sure you sink the hole in the true center. Properly centered clay doesn't wobble when the wheel is in motion.

Problem: The form is twisted.

Solution: A twist in the clay is the result of torque—an invisible force. There may be a thin spot in the wall of the pot that's causing it to collapse, either from the weight of too much clay at the rim or from a grip that was too strong when you pulled the walls. (Remember to ease off on the pressure as you pull upward.) To straighten twisted walls, compress the clay with your left hand on the inside and a metal rib on the outside.

Problem: There's too much clay at the bottom of the pot.

Solution: Start your pull a little more aggressively, from the bottom, where most of the clay is. As you pull, ease up on the pressure and follow through all the way to the top of the cylinder wall.

Technique: **Pulling a Handle**

Great handles are both comfortable to hold and visually balanced. A pulled handle is made in a way that subtly complements a wheel-thrown pot because both the handle and pot have been formed quickly by wetting and stretching the clay. Aesthetically, a handle is said to "interact" with a pot's form, so both form and function guide the handle-making process. A beer stein, for example, calls for a substantial, full-fist-sized handle, while a teacup only needs a handle large enough to accommodate one finger.

◼ VERTICAL HANDLES

The clay for a handle is attached to a pot when the pot is leather hard. To attach any two pieces of clay, you must first *score* and *slip* them. Scoring roughens the surfaces, while slip, which is very wet clay, acts as glue. **1** To make your own slip, see the instructions in Handy and Homemade, on page 120. To practice, use the instructions that follow to adhere several handles onto a single pot.

> ▶ **Tip:** As your pots await handles, cover them with plastic to keep them from drying out too much. If necessary, spray them lightly with water to remoisten them.

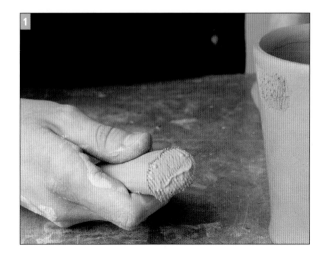

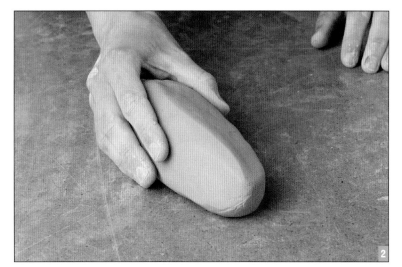

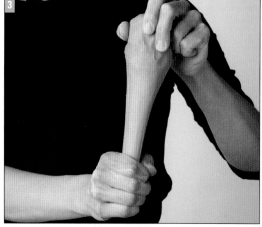

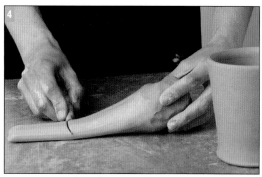

To make several mug-sized handles, first wedge 2 pounds (.9 kg) of clay. (Just adjust the amount as necessary, depending on the sizes and number of the mugs you're working with.) Then tap and rotate one end of the clay on the table to create a taper. **2**

Hold up the clay by its fat end, with the tapered end pointing toward the floor. Wet your other hand and grip the tapered area with it. To extend the handle, make a few pulls downward by squeezing gently with your gripping hand; apply most of the pressure in the area where your thumb and index finger encircle the clay. As you pull, your hand should glide down along the clay coil. **3** To maintain an even handle thickness, change your pulling hand's position on the clay with each successive pull. Throughout this process, you'll have to wet the pulling hand frequently so that it continues to slide over the clay. If the clay tears, you're using too much pressure. Just start over with the rest of the clay.

Next, use a needle to cut a *lug* (a short section of clay) from the pulled coil. **4** For a mug, a small lug is typically about 3 inches (7.6 cm) long and about ¾ inch (1.9 cm) thick; lugs for larger handles are longer and thicker. The cross section of the lug (at left) shows that the clay has been pulled to an oval profile rather than a round one.

One end of the lug must be securely attached to the mug so that you can continue the pulling process that will form the handle. Using a serrated rib, score both the thick end of the lug and the area on the mug where you'd like the handle to begin. Then apply dabs of slip to one of the scored areas. Holding one hand inside the mug for support, wiggle and press the slipped end of the lug onto the piece. **5** Then wet your hand, and use your thumb and index finger to work clay from all around the lug into the wall of the mug. The lug should be thick enough and short enough to stand straight off the pot.

Hold the mug so that the handle hangs straight down. Wet your other hand and continue pulling, just as you did to make the lug. **6** Apply more pressure at the top, where the clay is thick; as you near the end of your pull, release the pressure completely. Doing this creates a thick-to-thin-to-thick profile; thick handle ends are desirable for secure attachment to the mug. A mug handle should be about ½ inch (1.3 cm) thick and about 4 inches (10.2 cm) long.

Tip the mug upright, supporting the handle and arching it into a curve as you do. **7** To determine the placement of the other end of your handle, eyeball both the handle's profile and the mug's. Be sure to look at the handle head-on, too, so that you mount it to the pot on a true vertical line. When you're satisfied with the handle's position, press its free end into the pot, just enough to make it stick, and use your needle to cut away any excess clay. **8** Adjust the curve of your handle further, if desired. **9**

Use a wet thumb to rock and press the end of the handle securely into the pot. **10** Then smooth and clean the surrounding areas with one fingernail. Use a dampened brush to smooth out the clay and remove any fingerprints. **11**

▶ **Video Tip:** To see a video of me attaching a pulled handle to a mug, visit www.larkbooks. com/crafts.

■ HORIZONTAL HANDLES

Pairs of horizontal handles work well for low, wide pieces such as colanders, serving dishes, and bowls. To make them, follow the basic procedure for pulling vertical handles, but focus on keeping both ends equally thick and the mid-section slightly thinner. After pulling your first lug, cut it to 3 inches (7.6 cm) in length, or to any length you'd like, and set it aside. Pull the second lug and cut it to the same length. 12

Place your pot on a banding wheel. Score two areas for the ends of one handle, just under the rim, placing them 2 inches (5 cm) apart—or a distance 1 inch (2.5 cm) less than the handle's overall length. Score the underside ends of the handle, apply slip to them, and lightly press them onto the scored areas. Holding one hand on the inside of the pot for support, work each end of the handle onto the pot by rocking a wet thumb back and forth over it. 13

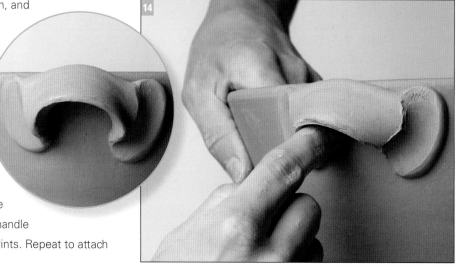

To shape the handle into an attractive curve, wet your index finger, and run it back and forth along the underside, lifting the outside edge as you do. 14 Smooth over the handle with a damp brush to remove fingerprints. Repeat to attach the other handle.

Project: **Mug**

My definition of a great mug is one that holds just the right amount of coffee, can be sipped from easily, and has a comfortable handle with a good fit. This first project is based on the basic cylinder form you just learned how to throw, but with a little ingenuity and practice, it can be so much more.

▲ **Tools**
Serrated rib, stamp
(optional; see page 121)

▶ **Tip:** Start with 1 pound (.45 kg) of well-wedged clay for the mug's body, and ½ pound (.23 kg) for the handle.

1 Center and throw a cylinder. To create the convex curve in the form, you'll use a metal rib. With the fingertips of your left hand inside the pot, about halfway down, gently push the wall out while making contact on the outside with the flexed edge of the rib. (While you're shaping this piece, your wheel speed should be slow to medium.)

2 To create the concave curve toward the top of the cylinder, use the rib to apply pressure from the outside, one-third of the way down, while resisting the pressure with your fingers inside.

3 Refine the rim by holding the straight edge of the rib against the rim on the inside, angling it into the pot. Place your left thumb opposite to the rib, on the outside of the rim. Gently compress the rim between the rib and your thumb, creating a bevel for comfortable sipping. If the rib trims away some of the clay instead of compressing it, ease up on the pressure.

4 To smooth the clay, drape a chamois over the rim, and hold it in place with both hands while the wheel makes several rotations. No pressure is necessary.

▶ **Tip:** All sorts of ordinary objects, as well as bisque stamps (page 121), can be used to create texture on clay: buttons, bark, nuts, and kitchen gizmos, for example. Those that work best are made of materials such as wood that won't stick to the clay easily. To keep a plastic, metal, or glass stamp from sticking, dust the surface of the pot with a little baby powder before stamping.

5 To make decorative impressions—an optional step—support the inside of the mug with one hand as you press a stamp or small object into the outer wall. Roll the object around slightly to make sure the impression is a good one. Repeat as many times as desired.

6 Use a wooden modeling tool to cut a channel at the base of the mug, release the mug from the wheel head with a wire tool, and transfer it by hand to a ware board to dry. Invert the mug when the rim has stiffened, and allow the bottom to dry to leather hard.

A transparent glaze was applied with a brush to the stamped areas of the bisque-fired mug. Wax was applied on top of the stamped areas, the interior was lined with a transparent glaze, and the exterior was dipped in a matte green glaze before glaze firing.

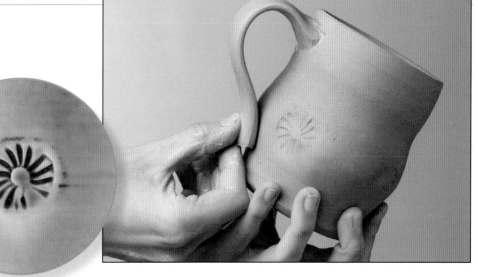

7 Roll the bottom edge of the mug on a table, then thumb over it to make it smooth. Make a lug, and pull a handle off the mug for a fresh, soft look.

Project: **Pitcher**

The challenge of making a pitcher is to create one that's relatively large, but not too heavy. Consider proportion and parts. How large should the pot be, and where should the handle go? A curving, voluptuous form leaves a negative space over which a handle can soar, ending at the hip. Keep the rim narrow and the handle just large enough for your hand. Here, you'll learn how to make a spout that delivers liquid smoothly, without dripping.

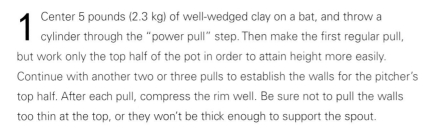

▲ Tools
Foam, serrated rib

1 Center 5 pounds (2.3 kg) of well-wedged clay on a bat, and throw a cylinder through the "power pull" step. Then make the first regular pull, but work only the top half of the pot in order to attain height more easily. Continue with another two or three pulls to establish the walls for the pitcher's top half. After each pull, compress the rim well. Be sure not to pull the walls too thin at the top, or they won't be thick enough to support the spout.

RELATED TECHNIQUES

▶ **Tip:** To put less strain on your wrists when centering a large amount of clay, as you must when making this pitcher, position your right shoulder over the clay, and use your body weight to help you.

2 Now work the bottom half of the pitcher with two or three pulls, moving from the bottom to halfway up the body.

3 Compress and shape the walls between your fingertips and a rib. To help shape your pitcher, grip the tool firmly, holding it angled away from you and against the pot.

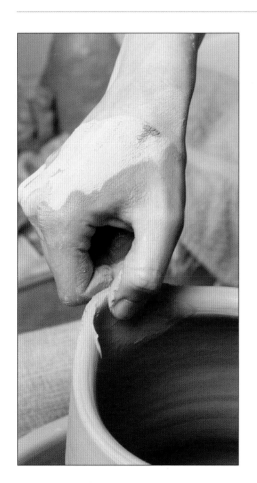

4 The spout is made by pulling clay from the rim. Wet your dominant hand and grip the rim, with your thumb inside the pot and the edge of your index finger on the outside. Pull the clay 1 inch (2.5 cm) or so below the rim, gently pinching the clay as you do. Don't pull to the very edge; release the pressure just before the spout's tip so that it doesn't become too flimsy and weak. Make several pulls, working back and forth along the rim, in an area about 2 to 3 inches (5 to 7.6 cm) wide.

▶ **Tip:** Smaller pitchers, such as creamers and gravy boats, can be made in the same way as large ones, using smaller amounts of clay. There's no need for a bat when throwing the smaller forms.

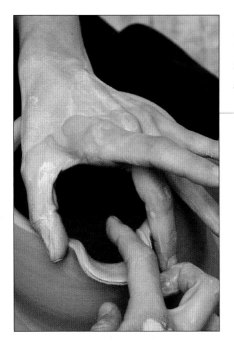

5 Rest a thumb and finger on either side of the outside of the spout. Position your other index finger, wetted, inside it, pointing into the pot. While supporting the outside of the spout, gently press and rock the inside finger back and forth across its width, working the clay downward as you do.

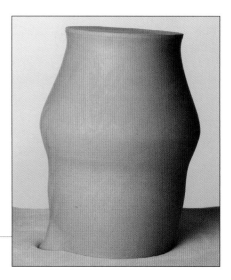

6 Cut a channel at the foot of the pitcher, and release it from the wheel head with a wire tool. Remove the bat and allow your pitcher to dry until the rim begins to stiffen to the leather-hard stage. Then invert the pitcher on a piece of foam, and allow the base to dry.

7 Cup the pitcher's sides in your hands, and roll its bottom edge on a flat surface. Smooth the clay with your thumb; no water is necessary.

8 To finish your pitcher, pull a handle directly opposite to the spout. (The size of the handle should be relative to the pitcher's size.)

The bottom half of this pitcher was first dipped in terra-cotta-colored glaze. Wax resist was brushed on top of the glaze in a spiral pattern. After the wax dried, the bottom half of the piece was dipped again, this time in a matte green glaze. The top half was dipped in a runny blue glaze, and the piece was fired to a high temperature.

Project: **Fluted Oval Baker**

Thrown pots don't have to be round. After the initial shaping process, the form of this baking dish is *altered* while the dish is off the wheel. Altering (modifying a round, thrown form) the soft, just-thrown clay is sure to inspire you. A bottomless cylinder becomes an oval, to which you attach a slab—and you've created a fabulous baking dish. To make small hot-dip bakers or large lasagna bakers, just adjust the size of the starting cylinder.

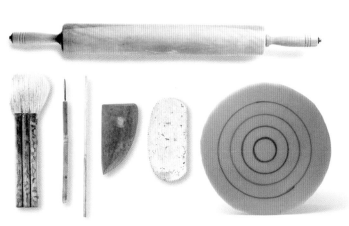

▲ **Tools**

Rolling pin, brush, small knife, chopstick, wooden rib, serrated rib, foam bat

1 Center 2 pounds (.9 kg) of well-wedged clay on a bat. Use the heel of your palm to work the clay out from the center, so it's centered low and wide— about 5 to 6 inches (12.7 to 15.2 cm) in diameter. Sink a centered hole all the way to the bat.

2 With your hands at the six o'clock position and your fingertips curled back and close to the bat, pull the clay toward your body to open up the hole. This creates a ring of clay approximately 2 inches (5 cm) thick.

3 With your left hand, use a claw-like grip at the six o'clock position to make a power pull. As you do this, your left thumb should grip the bottom of the clay firmly, outside the wall, while the fingers inside resist; your right hand should rest on top of your left.

4 Make regular pulls to throw a cylinder about 3½ inches (8.9 cm) tall, flaring it slightly at the rim. Compress the rim after each pull, leaving it nice and round. Leave the walls about ½ inch (1.3 cm) thick for fluting later.

5 Use a metal rib to compress the walls and smooth away the throwing marks. At the same time, angle the rib outward at the rim, compressing the clay against it to create the final, flared shape.

6 Holding a wooden modeling tool as if it were a pencil and using only slight pressure, create subtle detail by making an impression in the rim while the wheel rotates.

7 To flute the form, stop the wheel and hold your left hand against the inside wall of the pot. Hold a wooden rib in your other hand, and dip its square edge in water. Gently press the corner of the rib into the base of the pot, while holding your left hand on the inside to resist the pressure. Simultaneously lift both your left hand and the wooden rib toward the rim, while maintaining a gentle pressure with the tool. Rotate the wheel slightly, and repeat to make flutes all the way around your cylinder. Notice how the line on the split rim undulates after fluting.

8 Using a wooden modeling tool, cut a channel at the base of the cylinder, and release it with a wire tool. Remove the bat from the wheel, and let the cylinder set up until it's no longer tacky but not yet leather hard—for an hour or less, depending on the humidity. To form an oval, gently lift one side of the cylinder to loosen it, and pull it toward the edge of the bat. Do the same at the opposite side. Refine the ends of the oval by compressing the walls between the palms of your hands.

9 Set the cylinder aside while you make a slab. Cut a 2-inch-thick (5 cm) slice from a block of clay, and toss it, at an angle, onto a ware board. (Angling the toss stretches the clay.) Repeat to toss it again. Set a matching pair of ⅜-inch-square (1 cm) dowels on opposing sides of the slab, leaving a couple of inches (5 cm) between each dowel and the clay. Roll over the slab with a rolling pin until the rolling pin passes smoothly over the dowels, with no resistance from the clay. Let the slab dry to the soft leather-hard stage.

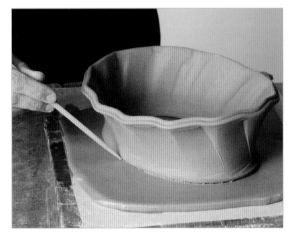

10 When the rim of the cylinder is stiff enough for you to pick it up without distorting it, turn it upside down and rest it on a foam bat until the base has dried to the soft leather-hard stage. The slab should be at the same stage of dryness. Carefully place the cylinder on top of the slab, right side up. Use a chopstick to mark the slab, around the outside edge of the cylinder.

11 Remove the cylinder. Then use a small knife to cut along the mark you've made on the slab, and remove the excess clay.

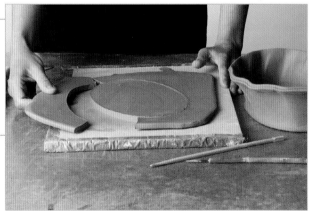

12 Use a serrated rib to score both the bottom edge of your cylinder and the area of the slab that the cylinder will contact when the two pieces are joined. Then brush slip (see page 120) onto the scored base of the cylinder. Turn the cylinder right side up and press it gently down onto the slab, matching the scored areas carefully.

13 Work clay from the base of the cylinder into the slab. Then sandwich the piece between the ware board and a foam bat, and flip the bat and board over to turn the piece upside down.

14 Use a rubber rib to smooth and compress the slab against the cylinder, and round the edge by flexing the rib over it. Then flip your baker upright for drying.

▶ **Tip:** Avoid "shocking" your finished baker! Never transfer cold ceramic ware straight from the fridge to a hot oven. Let the ware warm to room temperature first, or preheat it slowly in the oven.

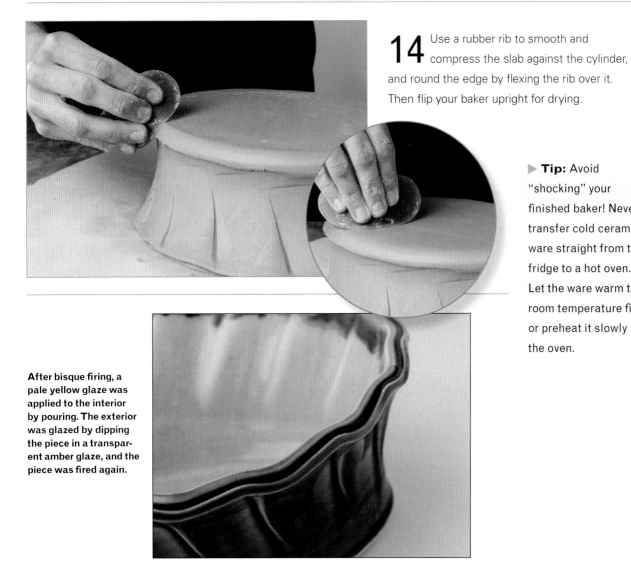

After bisque firing, a pale yellow glaze was applied to the interior by pouring. The exterior was glazed by dipping the piece in a transparent amber glaze, and the piece was fired again.

Gallery: Cylinder-Based Forms

Silvie Granatelli
Mugs, 2008

4½ x 3½ x 3½ inches (11.4 x 8.9 x 8.9 cm)
Wheel-thrown porcelain; dipped and sprayed glaze; carving;
gas fired, cone 10
Photo by Molly Selznick

Kristen Kieffer
Cordial Cups, 2008

2½ x 2 inches (6.4 x 5 cm)
Thrown and altered porcelain; dipped glaze; stamping, slip trailing;
electric fired, cone 7
Photo by artist

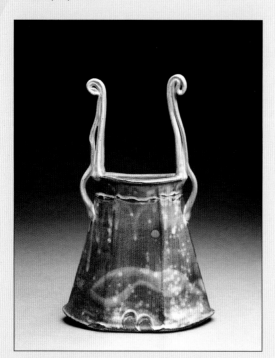

Matt Kelleher
Mimi Vase, 2008

10 x 7 x 5 inches (25.4 x 17.8 x 12.7 cm)
Thrown and altered stoneware; poured slip glaze; faceting; soda
fired, cone 10
Photo by artist

Bradley C. Birkhimer
Oval Pitchers, 2008

12½ x 12 x 7 inches (31.8 x 30.5 x 17.8 cm)
Thrown and altered porcelaneous stoneware; nuka ash
liner; waxed with poured porcelain and trailed ash glaze;
wood fired with salt and soda, cone 11
Photo by artist

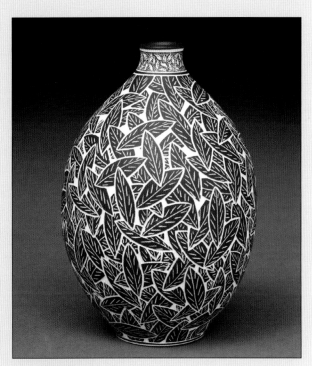

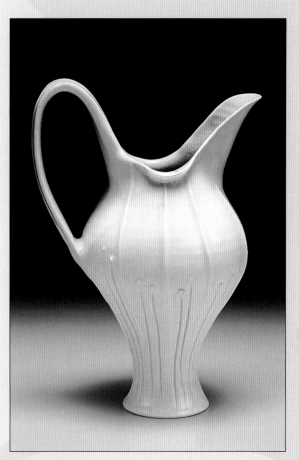

Becky Lloyd
Steve Lloyd
Bottle, 2008

5 x 3 x 3 inches (12.7 x 7.6 x 7.6 cm)
Wheel-thrown porcelain; brushed glaze; sgraffito, terra
sigillata; electric fired, cone 10
Photo by artist

Leah Leitson
Pitcher, 2006

8 x 7¼ x 6½ inches (20.3 x 18.4 x 16.5 cm)
Thrown and altered porcelain; sprayed glaze; applied clay; electric
fired, cone 6
Photo by Tim Barnwell

Stanley Mace Andersen
Yunomis, 2006

4 x 3½ x 3½ inches (10.2 x 8.9 x 8.9 cm)
Wheel-thrown earthenware; dipped glaze;
maiolica technique; electric fired, cone 03
Photo by Tom Mills

Marty Fielding
Mug, 2008

3¾ x 4¾ x 3½ inches (9.5 x 12.1 x 8.9 cm)
Wheel-thrown earthenware; brushed glaze; inlaid slip, terra sigil-
lata; electric fired, cone 04
Photo by artist

Jason Bohnert
Pair of Mugs, 2008

4 x 3 x 4 inches (10.2 x 7.6 x 10.2 cm)
Wheel-thrown white stoneware; dipped glaze; underglaze
brushwork; gas, wood and soda fired, cone 10/11
Photo by artist

Kyle Carpenter
Mug, 2007

3½ x 2¾ x 3¾ inches (8.9 x 7 x 9.5 cm)
Wheel-thrown stoneware; dipped flashing slip glaze; glaze brush-
work, underglaze brushwork; salt-fired gas, cone 9
Photo by Tim Barnwell

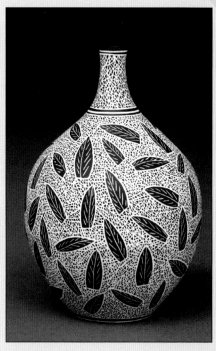

Brooke Noble
Tumblers, 2008

7½ x 4 x 4 inches (19 x 10.2 x 10.2 cm)
Wheel-thrown porcelain; brushed, sprayed, dipped,
needle bottle glaze; carved, inlaid slip, underglaze
brushwork, underglaze pencils, screen printing,
overglaze; gas fired in soda, cone 10
Photo by artist

Becky Lloyd
Steve Lloyd
Bottle, 2008

8 x 4½ x 4½ inches (20.3 x 11.4 x 11.4 cm)
Wheel-thrown porcelain; brushed glaze; sgraffito, terra
sigilatta; electric fired, cone 10
Photo by artist

Shoko Teruyama
Matt Kelleher
Bird Vase, 2008

17 x 14 x 14 inches (43.2 x 35.6 x 35.6 cm)
Thrown and altered earthenware; brushed glaze;
sgraffito; electric fired, cone 04
Photo by Matt Kelleher

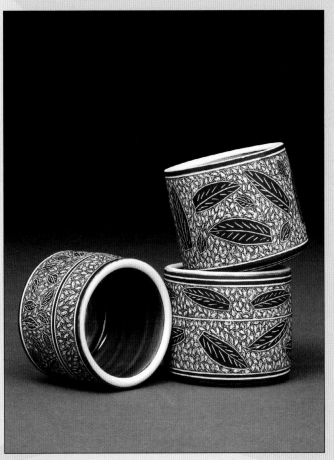

Becky Lloyd
Steve Lloyd
Sake Cups, 2008

2¼ x 2 x 2 inches (6.4 x 5 x 5 cm)
Wheel-thrown porcelain; brushed glaze; sgraffito, terra sigilatta;
electric fired, cone 10
Photo by artist

Lindsay Rogers
Two Mugs, 2008

7 x 3 x 3 inches (17.8 x 7.6 x 7.6 cm)
Wheel-thrown stoneware; porcelain slip, sgraffito, oxide wash;
wood/salt fired, cone 10
Photo by Marisa Falcigno

Lisa Naples
Crow Cup, 2008

3¾ x 5¾ x 4 inches (9.5 x 14.6 x 10.2 cm)
Wheel-thrown earthenware; dipped glaze; underglaze
brushwork, dry brushed slips over scratched texture;
electric fired
Photo by Jim Greipp

Technique: **Throwing a Bowl**

Simply put, a bowl is a form that's wider at its rim than it is at its foot. Its walls generally rise out of the base as a continuous and uninterrupted curve. Unlike a cylinder, the walls of a bowl aren't usually thrown to a uniform thickness; walls that are thicker near the base help to support the bowl's curve so that it doesn't collapse as you throw it. After the thrown piece has dried a bit, the excess clay at the bottom is trimmed to form a foot ring.

▧ PULLING THE BOWL

Place several 2-pound (.9 kg) balls of wedged clay and the necessary tools within arm's reach. Center one piece of clay on the wheel, and sink a hole, as you would for a cylinder. **1** Check the thickness of the bottom with your needle tool; it should be about 1 inch (2.5 cm).

▶ **Tip:** Some of the projects in this book require throwing large amounts of clay. When you're first learning to make pots, start off small and work your way up to larger pieces.

With a bowl form, you open the hole while simultaneously making a power pull. Use your left hand, at the six o'clock position, to take a grip on the clay, and rest your right hand on top of your left. Rotate your left wrist slightly and apply pressure with your thumb at the base. **2** As you pull the clay upward and outward, continue applying pressure with your thumb, while resisting that pressure with your fingertips on the interior. **3** Ease off on the pressure as you near the rim.

To keep the rim from getting too thin and cracking under the stress of stretching, pinch it with your left thumb and index finger at the six o'clock position, while resting your right index finger on the rim and crossing the fingers of your left hand to form a letter H. **4** Don't press or pinch hard; just rest your finger on the rim for a few rotations of the wheel.

Next, make two or three regular pulls at the three to four o'clock position, with your left fingers inside the pot and the fingertips of your right hand outside. **5** When you throw a cylinder, your outside (right) hand dominates, but when you throw a bowl, it's your inside (left) hand that creates the pressure necessary to move the walls outward. Pulling a bowl may feel a little awkward at first, but with practice you'll learn how to apply the pressure correctly. Think of your inside hand as making a sweeping motion against the interior of the bowl, and remember that your pulls should be upward and outward. Employing the two opposing forces of both hands helps to maintain a smooth inside curve.

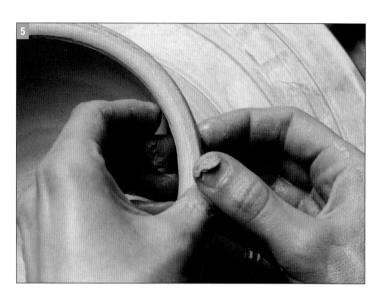

▶ **Tip:** The interior of a bowl is said to contain its soul. Focus on creating the interior form and curve while you're throwing. Refining the exterior form comes later, during trimming.

■ FINISHING THE BOWL

To refine the bowl's curve, hold a metal rib in your right hand, and position it just inside the rim of the pot, at the six o'clock position. Twist your left wrist so that your palm faces the outside of the bowl, opposite to the rib in your right hand. **6** Run the wide edge of the rib gently along the inside of your bowl, starting at the rim and ending in the center. Your left hand simply supports the outside wall during this step.

Cut a groove with a wooden modeling tool at the base of the bowl. **7** Release the bowl with a wire tool, dry your hands, and make sure you have a ware board near the wheel.

▶ **Video Tip:** To watch a video of me throwing a bowl from 2 pounds (.9 kg) of clay, visit www.larkbooks.com/crafts.

Position each hand, palm down, on one side of the bowl. Gripping its base with your thumbs and index fingers, twist the bowl slightly and lift it off the wheel. **8** Don't worry if your fingers dent the clay a bit as you lift. If you've left enough clay on the base, the pot itself won't be distorted. If you do make a small dent in the pot, just push it back out with one finger. Let the bowl dry until its rim stiffens; then invert it and allow the base to become leather hard before moving on to the next step—trimming.

■ CUTTING A CROSS SECTION

After each of your first few attempts at throwing a bowl, cut a cross section through the pot and study its thickness throughout. **9** **10** Extravagant as this process may seem, it will help you focus on the areas in which you need improvement. The rim of the bowl at the top of photo 9, for example, is too thin, and its interior curve is uneven. The base of the bowl at the bottom has too little clay to support its wide diameter. The bowl in photo 10 is what you're aiming for: its rim is strong, its curve is even and graceful, and its base has enough clay to make trimming a foot ring possible. For solutions to the most common throwing problems, see Troubleshooting on page 34.

▶ **Tip:** A bowl thrown with more than 4 pounds (1.8 kg) of clay is difficult to remove from the wheel without distorting it. Throw a large bowl on a bat instead, release it with a wire tool, and allow it to dry on the bat until its rim stiffens and it can be inverted for further drying.

Technique: **Trimming**

Trimming, which is done at the leather-hard stage, is the process of cutting away excess clay from the base of a pot in order to create a foot ring and uniformly thick walls. It's executed with a sharp tool while the inverted pot spins on the wheel, and the true form of the piece you've thrown is revealed in the process. The foot ring provides a nice finishing touch and also reduces the exposed surface area at the bottom of the pot so that less clay will come in contact with any surface the pot sits on.

■ EVALUATING AND SETTING UP

The rim is the first area to become stiff as a pot dries. Once the rim has stiffened, invert the pot so that the remaining areas dry evenly until the entire pot is leather hard.

Before you start trimming, hold the pot in your hands. Feel its weight, take note of its wall thickness and base, and decide which areas need to be trimmed and how you'll need to change the base's profile so that the curve of the exterior walls matches that of the pot's interior. Potters often strive to make the foot ring the same width as the thickness of a pot's walls. Figure 5 shows cross sections of an inverted pot before and after trimming.

▶ **Video Tip:** To watch a video of me trimming a pot, visit www.larkbooks.com/crafts.

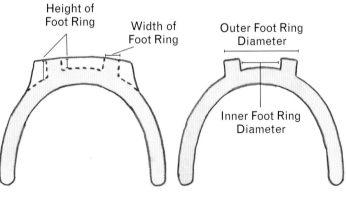

Height of Foot Ring

Width of Foot Ring

Outer Foot Ring Diameter

Inner Foot Ring Diameter

Figure 5

Place your pot, upside down, in the center of the wheel head, using the concentric rings as guides. **1** Rotate the wheel head slowly to check that the pot is centered; it won't wobble if it is. If the pot is slightly off center, hold a steady finger next to—but not quite touching—its base, while the wheel rotates at a slow speed. **2** Stop the wheel when the pot touches your finger, and tap the pot away from you, in the opposite direction. Repeat this process until the rotating pot stays in continuous contact with your steady finger.

Next, while holding the pot in place with your left hand, affix it to the wheel head with three small coils of clay, placed at equal distances. **3** Moisten one side of each coil and press that side down onto the wheel head (not onto the pot's edge), where the pot and wheel head meet. Be careful: pushing the coil into the pot may distort its rim.

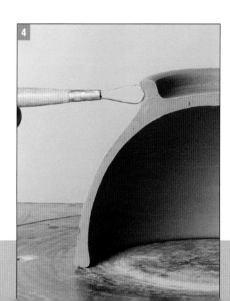

■ ESTABLISHING A FOOT RING

The edges of trimming tools come in different shapes; the one you choose can help to establish your pot's profile. Ribbon tools with flat or curved shapes are very useful. **4** **5** For trimming, I usually use a pear-shaped ribbon tool with one flat edge, one curved edge, and a pointed end that make it versatile for trimming different areas of a pot.

▶ **Tip:** To help secure a vertical pot for trimming, use a sponge to make a ring of moisture on the wheel head, and position the rim of the pot on top of it; the water will create a seal between the wheel head and rim. Affix the pot with large coils of clay. Some vertical forms can only be trimmed using a chuck (see page 119).

▶ **Tip:** Use a slightly faster wheel speed for trimming than you'd use for throwing. Quick spinning allows you to cut through irregularities and remove excess clay aggressively.

Hold the tool in your right hand, at the four o'clock position, and rest your left hand on the pot. To help stabilize the tool, bridge your hands with your left thumb. Position the tool so that its pointed end contacts the pot just below the edge of the base. As the wheel spins, apply pressure with the pointed end, and as you maintain that pressure, gradually adjust the tool's cutting angle to remove the desired amount of clay. **6** Removing this clay establishes the height of the foot ring, as well as its outer diameter. Coordinate the tool's pressure with the speed of the wheel; too much pressure at a slow speed—or too much at a high one—can cause you to cut the foot ring off center.

Next, use the flat edge of the tool to round out the area just below the foot so that its curve mirrors the interior curve of the pot. **7**

▶ **Tip:** If the trimmings reattach themselves to the pot, the pot is too wet. Let it dry a bit more before continuing. You'll also know your pot needs more drying time if its shape is easily distorted when you try to move it, or if fingerprints show up when you touch it. If you find it difficult to make a fingernail impression in the clay, or if you have to use a lot of pressure while trimming and your tool makes a high-pitched humming sound as you work, the pot is too close to the bone-dry stage to trim successfully.

▓ TRIMMING INSIDE THE FOOT RING

As the wheel rotates, use the pointed end of the tool to mark the thickness of the foot ring; it should be ¼ to ⅜ inch (6 mm to 1 cm). Then, with the same end of the tool angled at about 45°, apply pressure to dig into the clay where you marked. **8** Continue to trim away clay until the interior height of the foot ring matches its exterior height. To trim away the remaining clay inside the foot ring, run the tool from the edge of the ring to the center and back a few times, gradually decreasing the angle of the tool as you do. **9**

During trimming, grog in the clay is exposed on the pot's surface. To compress it back below the surface, while the wheel is in motion, run the edge of a rubber rib up and down the exterior of the pot and over the foot ring. **10**

Trimming away just the right amount of clay from the base of a pot can be tricky. If you haven't had much practice yet, trim just a little bit and then turn the pot over to check the thickness of the base from the inside before continuing. In time, gauging how much trimming is necessary will become easier. It's a good idea to have multiple pieces to trim in one sitting; if you accidentally trim through one base, you can keep practicing on the others.

Finally, leave your mark! Before you set your pot aside to dry, sign it—proudly—using either a dull pencil or a stamp (see page 121).

Project: **Plate**

A plate is simply a flat bowl with a continuous curve that's very subtle. The process of making one, however, is somewhat different. Because throwing a flat piece such as a plate stresses the clay particles, you compress the clay after establishing the interior so that the piece won't crack as it dries. You must also start out with more clay than you would for a bowl, and throw a thicker bottom. Why? Because as you release a flat piece from the bat, the wire tends to rise underneath it and remove clay from the bottom. A plate's true form is revealed when it's trimmed.

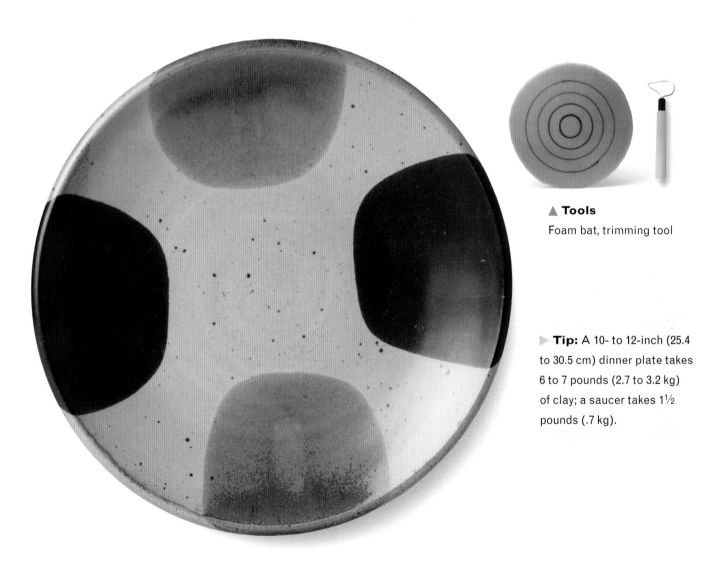

▲ **Tools**
Foam bat, trimming tool

▶ **Tip:** A 10- to 12-inch (25.4 to 30.5 cm) dinner plate takes 6 to 7 pounds (2.7 to 3.2 kg) of clay; a saucer takes 1½ pounds (.7 kg).

RELATED TECHNIQUES

1 Center the clay low and wide on a bat. When centering amounts of clay this large, set the wheel speed between medium and fast, and lean over the wheel, with your shoulder square above the clay. Allow the heel of your palm to create the indent that will begin the interior curve of your plate. To avoid trapping air underneath the clay, use the heel of your palm to apply pressure at the very center of the clay and spread it outward.

2 Use your fingertips to create the interior curve. Beginning in the center, apply pressure with them as if you were grabbing the clay, and maintain that pressure as you pull the clay mostly outward—and slightly upward at the rim. Check the thickness of the bottom with a needle tool; it should be $\frac{1}{2}$ to $\frac{3}{4}$ inch (1.3 to 1.9 cm).

3 Compress the clay by applying slight downward pressure with your fingertips as you move them from the edge to the center and back again. Repeat this a few times, keeping in mind that you're not pulling or moving the clay—just compressing it.

4 With the wheel rotating slowly, pull the walls of your plate, in much the same way as you would if you were pulling the walls of a bowl. You'll only need to make a couple of pulls, however—and be sure to pull outward more than upward.

5 For the final shaping, use the wide, curved edge of a metal rib to refine and clean the interior curve of the plate. Begin by pressing the tool against the rim. Apply slight pressure with it from the rim to the center, and then lift it away.

6 Use a wooden modeling tool to make a channel at the base of the plate. Release the plate from the bat with a wire tool, holding the wire taut. Remove the bat from the wheel, and let the plate's rim dry to leather hard. Then place a foam bat on top of the plate, and flip the bats over to invert it. (Never flip large plates without the added support of a bat on each side, or the plates could warp.) Remove the upper bat and allow the entire plate to dry to the hard leather-hard stage.

7 With the plate still inverted on the foam bat, trim a foot ring that's at least two-thirds the diameter of the rim. Because plates are low and wide, they should be trimmed at the hard leather-hard stage, with a sharp trimming tool. If the clay is too soft, the area inside the foot ring can collapse under the pressure of your tool.

After bisque firing, the entire plate was dipped in a matte white glaze. Matte black and transparent amber were poured on top.

Project: **Berry Bowl**

A berry bowl is simply a small colander. This design features a deep form and a tall foot that's trimmed at the leather-hard stage to allow water to drain well away from the bowl. Handles allow you to hold the bowl securely as you shake out the excess water. You'll throw this bowl form on a bat.

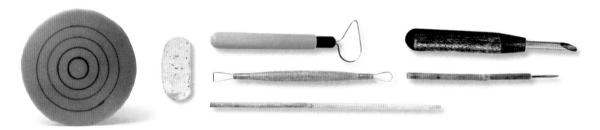

▲ **Tools**

Foam bat, serrated rib, hole-making tool, trimming tools, small knife, chopstick

▶ **Tip:** Try making your bowl with 3 to 6 pounds (1.4 to 2.7 kg) of clay.

RELATED TECHNIQUES

Centering	Throwing a Bowl	Trimming	Pulling a Handle (Horizontal Handles)	Handy and Homemade (Foam Bats)
26	**54**	**58**	**38**	**119**

1 Center the clay on a bat, creating an indentation in the middle of the clay with the heel of your right palm, while resting your left palm alongside the clay at the nine o'clock position. Leave plenty of clay in the bottom—at least 1 inch (2.5 cm)—for trimming a foot ring later. Throw a bowl, pulling upward and outward to create a deep form. For good control, keep the wheel speed slow and steady.

2 Holding a rib in each hand, compress and smooth the walls of the bowl. To smooth the rim, drape a chamois over it while the wheel rotates.

3 Use a wooden modeling tool to cut a channel at the base, and release the bowl with a wire tool. Lift the bat off the wheel, and allow the rim of the bowl to stiffen. Then place a foam bat on top of the bowl, and flip the two bats over to invert it. Remove the bat from the bottom of the bowl, and allow the bottom to dry to leather hard.

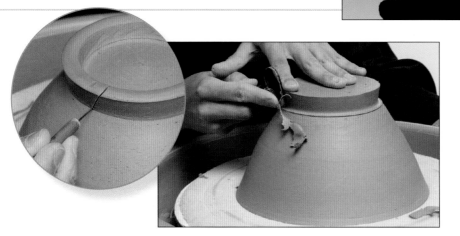

4 Attach a foam bat to your wheel, place the bowl on it, and trim a foot ring. To add visual interest, use a small knife to cut two to four triangular openings in the ring.

5 Take a look at the photo of the finished Berry Bowl on page 65. Its regular pattern of holes makes functionality visually appealing. Before creating similar holes in your own bowl, consider where you'd like to place them and how many you'd like to make in each set. To help position the holes evenly, first mark horizontal rings around the exterior of the bowl by holding a chopstick steadily against it as it rotates. Also mark a ring on the bottom of the bowl. Then mark locations on these rings for four, equidistant drainage holes in the bottom of the bowl and for the sets of holes in the wall.

6 To cut the marked holes, push the hole-making tool through the clay, twisting it as you do. Be sure to use a tool that's at least ⁵⁄₁₆ inch (8 mm) in diameter; glaze will clog holes that are much smaller.

7 Bevel both the inside and outside of each drainage hole with a narrow-looped trimming tool.

8 Pull two handles and attach them horizontally, just beneath the rim and opposite to each other.

Black underglaze was brushed onto the leather-hard surface. The bisque-fired bowl was dipped in a transparent blue glaze and immediately shaken to remove the excess, and the drainage holes were blown through to remove any glaze that might clog them. The bowl was then glaze fired.

Technique: **Decorating Surfaces**

The surface of an unfired pot can serve as a canvas for wonderfully expressive marks made with tools or brushes. Try one decorative technique on a single piece, or combine different approaches as a fun way to embellish your pots.

SGRAFFITO

Sgraffito is the process of etching through a layer of *underglaze* (a liquid ceramic pigment) or colored slip that you apply to the surface of a pot. After bisque firing, a transparent glaze is applied, for an appealing layered look, and the piece is fired again.

Commercial underglazes, which can be purchased through ceramic suppliers, come in a very wide variety of colors. To achieve more subtle colors, you may want to mix your own colored slips instead, by adding stains or colorants to a white slip (see Recipes on page 123).

Sgraffito can be done during either the wet or leather-hard stage. Simple, quickly made marks work well during the plastic stage, while highly detailed designs are better executed later so they won't get smudged while the clay is still malleable.

To create a quick, informal sgraffito design, use a wide brush with soft, long bristles to apply underglaze or colored slip to the pot, right after you've finished throwing it. Hold the brush against the piece as the wheel rotates slowly, and coat the area you want to decorate. **1** As the wheel continues to rotate, wiggle a serrated rib up and down to make wavy lines through the slip. **2**

For more formal designs with a lot of detail, apply underglaze or slip when the pot is leather hard. Affix your pot to the wheel head with coils of clay, or place it on a banding wheel; then brush on the underglaze or slip as the wheel rotates at a slow but steady speed. Alternatively, if you want to cover an entire piece with a colored slip that you've mixed yourself, dip your piece into the slip bucket. (For instructions on dipping, see step 9 on page 116.) Whether you dip or brush, allow the applied underglaze or slip to sit until it's dry to the touch. Then, with the piece on a banding wheel so you can work at eye level, use carving tools to etch through the brushed or dipped layer and expose the clay underneath. **3**

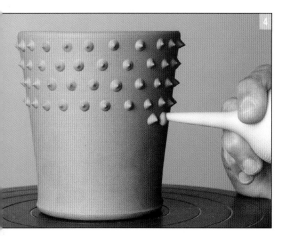

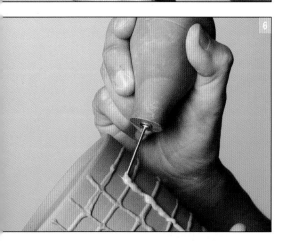

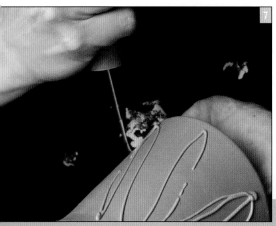

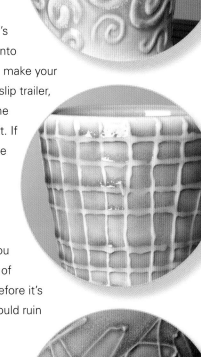

SLIP TRAILING

Slip trailing, which is similar to decorating a cake, offers innumerable ways to make a pot irresistibly touchable by adding texture to it. The slip that's used in this technique is thicker than slips applied by brushing or dipping. Unlike the latter, which are the consistency of heavy cream, the slip for trailing is more similar to yogurt and is almost appetizingly smooth and creamy. It's applied by squeezing it from a *slip trailer* onto the surface of a wet or leather-hard pot. To make your own thick slip, see page 120. To load your slip trailer, squeeze the air out of it, stick its tip into the slip, and allow suction to pull the slip into it. If this doesn't work, you may need to thin the slip a little.

Place a leather-hard pot on a banding wheel and squeeze out a repeated pattern of slip-trailed dots. **4** Alternatively, create lines in any pattern you like. **5 6 7** As you work, keep shaking the slip toward the tip of your trailer. Make sure to refill the trailer before it's empty, or it may trap a pocket of air that could ruin your design by causing the slip to splatter.

COMBING

Combing through wet slip with your fingers is another way to create a textured design. Start by throwing a pot on a bat so that the piece will be easy to remove later. Then brush a thick slip onto the pot while it's still wet and rotating on the wheel. **8** To create your design, run your fingers through the wet slip as the wheel rotates. **9**

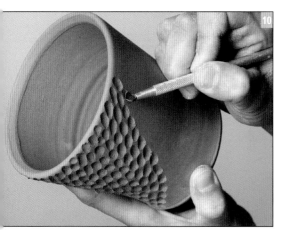

◼ CARVING

Carving designs in clay can be a quick, simple process or an involved, intricate one, but paired with the right glaze, any kind of carving can create attractive depth and texture on a pot's surface. Transparent glazes pool in the recessed areas and create subtle contrast between carved and uncarved areas. Experiment with different sizes and shapes of carving tools to create various types of line patterns—whether hard-edged, geometric, or soft and curving.

Carving is best done during the leather-hard stage, when the tool cuts through the clay like a knife through butter and leaves a clean mark. You may find it helpful to draw your design lightly on the pot before committing yourself to carving.

If you've ever made a linocut, you know that the cutting tool creates a three-dimensional groove in the soft ground. The same principle applies to clay-carving tools. To get a feel for how to maneuver the tool and how much pressure to apply, practice on a few pots. Following are a few techniques you may want to try.

Use a small, round loop tool to carve into the clay, lifting the tool out with a sweeping motion at the end of each cut. Repeat this quick, carved mark to mimic ripples of water. **10**

A dull pencil makes an excellent tool for carving subtle, shallow lines. Brush off any burrs only after the piece is bone dry. **11**

An L-shaped carving tool makes lines that look like pleated fabric. Cut a vertical line, holding the tool so that its corner makes a deep cut along one edge and lifting it out of the clay as you reach the end of the cut. Repeat to create as many lines as you like. **12**

A serrated tool carves a series of parallel lines all at once. To create a checkered pattern, carve short marks to make squares, alternating the directions of the lines in each square. **13**

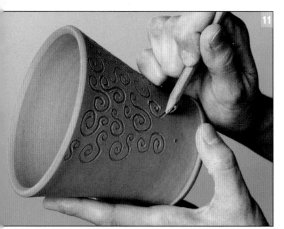

▦ INLAY

Inlay is a technique in which lines are scratched into the surface of the clay and then filled with colored slip or underglaze. When the slip or underglaze has dried, the excess is scraped from the surface to reveal the details of your pattern in the recessed lines. In a sense, inlay is just the opposite of sgraffito.

Carve a simple line pattern into the surface of a leather-hard pot. **14** Then brush colored slip or underglaze into the lines you've created, letting it overflow a bit. **15** After the slip or underglaze has dried to the touch, use the edge of a metal rib to scrape away the excess from the raised surfaces. **16** Remove the scrapings with a dry brush, bisque fire your inlaid piece, glaze it with a transparent glaze that won't mask the line work, and fire it again.

Project: **Flower Bowl**

This shallow bowl has a wide, flat rim that's ideal for decorative cutting. Because the form is so much wider than it is tall, it must be structurally supported with a curved wall and a sturdy, wide foot.

I threw this single serving dish with 4 pounds (1.8 kg) of clay. For a soap dish, use 1 pound (.5 kg); for a large serving bowl, use 12 pounds (5.4 kg).

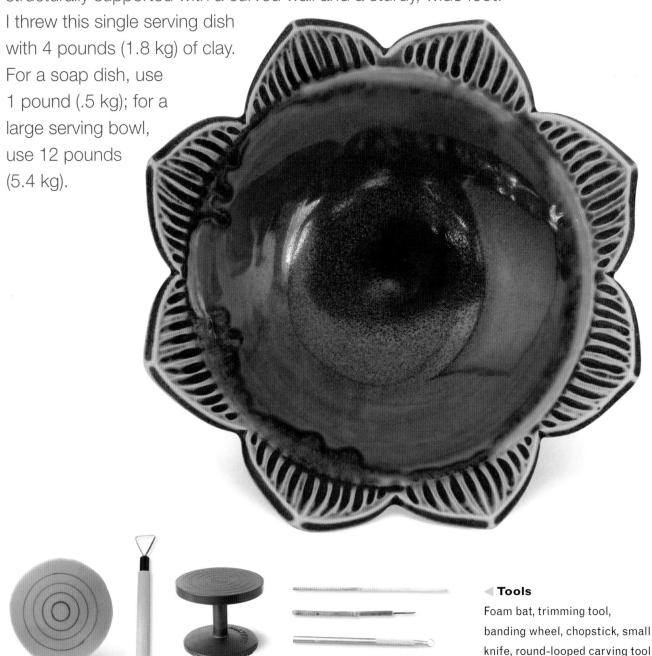

Tools
Foam bat, trimming tool, banding wheel, chopstick, small knife, round-looped carving tool

RELATED TECHNIQUES

Centering	Throwing a Bowl	Trimming	Handy and Homemade (Foam Bats)	Decorating Surfaces (Carving)
26	**54**	**58**	**119**	**72**

1 For shallow bowls, center the clay low and wide on a regular bat. To avoid trapping air underneath the clay, use the heel of your palm to apply pressure at the very center of the clay and spread it outward. Also use the heel of your palm to sink a hole in the middle.

2 Use your fingertips to compress and refine the hollow, and create a gradual interior curve. Leave 1 inch (2.5 cm) of clay at the base to be trimmed later.

3 Throw a bowl, pulling the walls outward more than upward. Keep the walls thick, and compress the rim.

4 To create the wide, flat rim, hold a metal rib in your right hand, with its flat edge against the interior rim of the pot. Support the underside of the rim with your left palm while applying a gentle downward pressure with the rib.

▶ **Tip:** To maintain a low, wide form, remember to use your inside (left) hand as the dominant force while you throw. Keep your wheel speed relatively slow, and make sure the base of the clay stays wide enough to support the width and curve of the piece.

5 Using the rounded edge of a metal rib, clean and refine the interior curve of the bowl. Then cut a channel at the base with a wooden modeling tool, and release the bowl with a wire tool. Remove the bat from the wheel, and when the rim has stiffened, invert your bowl and allow it to dry to leather hard.

6 Place the bowl on a foam bat, and trim a foot ring that's about two-thirds the diameter of the rim.

7 After trimming the foot, sandwich the bowl between two bats, flip it right side up, and place it on a banding wheel. Now you'll make guide marks to help you cut the decorative rim shapes. Using a chopstick, make eight evenly spaced marks around the inside edge of the rim. (These marks represent the tips of the petal-like shapes that you'll cut.) Also make eight marks in the middle of the flat portion of the rim, centering each one between the marks on the edge. (These interior marks represent the points at which the petal shapes join one another.)

8 Using a small knife, cut the petal-like shapes around the rim. Start at a mark on the edge of the rim, run the knife to a mark in the interior, and then run it out to the next mark on the edge, working around the entire rim. If you find that cutting through the clay is difficult, drape a damp (not wet) towel over the bowl for 10 minutes or so, then try again.

9 Use a damp chamois to soften the edges of your cuts.

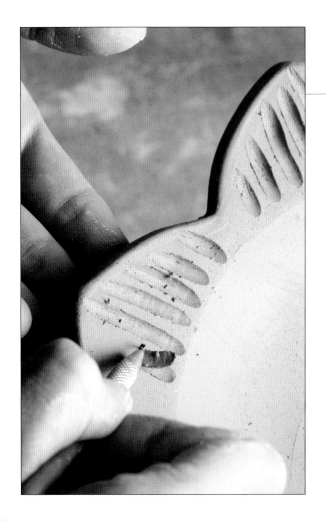

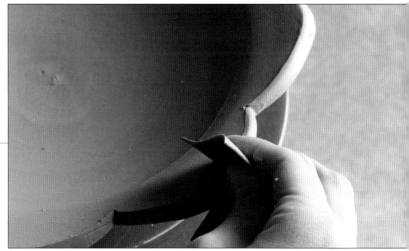

10 On each of the petal shapes, use a round loop-carving tool to carve several parallel lines. As you do this, be sure to support the underside of the petal with your free hand.

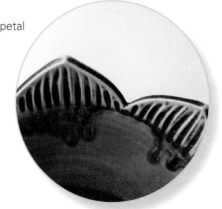

After bisque firing, a transparent amber glaze was poured on the inside and covered with wax resist. The entire piece was then dipped in a matte turquoise glaze and fired again.

Gallery: Bowl-Based Forms

Kristen Kieffer
Stamped Bowls, 2008

3½ x 5½ inches (8.9 x 14 cm)
Thrown and altered porcelain; dipped glaze; stamping, slip trailing;
electric fired, cone 7
Photo by artist

Jason Bohnert
Stacking Soup Bowls, 2008

3 x 5 x 6 inches (7.6 x 12.7 x 15.2 cm)
Wheel-thrown white stoneware; dipped glaze; faceting; wood/soda
fired, cone 10/11
Photo by artist

Kelly O'Briant
Peas Popping Serving Bowl, 2008

5 x 10 inches (12.7 x 25.4 cm)
Wheel-thrown and trimmed porcelain; dipped glaze;
underglaze brushwork, overglaze; electric fired, cone 6
Photo by Tom Mills

Marty Fielding
Platter, 2008

3 x 18 x 18 inches (7.6 x 45.7 x 45.7 cm)
Wheel-thrown stoneware; brushed and dipped glaze; wax resist;
gas fired, cone 10
Photo by artist

LeAnne Ash
Dinner Plate, 2008

2 x 10 x 10 inches (5 x 25.4 x 25.4 cm)
Thrown and altered stoneware; dipped glaze; wax
brushwork; gas fired, cone 10
Photo by Tom Mills

Benjamin Carter
Flower Brick Centerpiece, 2007

12 x 12 x 12 inches (30.5 x 30.5 x 30.5 cm)
Thrown and altered porcelain; dipped glaze;
residual soda; soda fired in gas kiln in reduction,
cone 10
Photo by artist

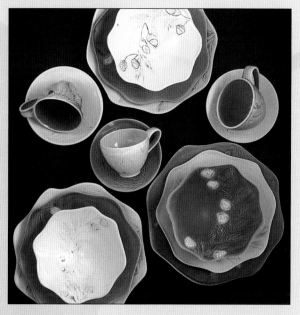

Silvie Granatelli
Wavy Dinnerware, 2007

Dinner Plate: 2 x 10 x 10 inches
(5 x 25.4 x 25.4 cm)
Thrown and altered porcelain; dipped glaze;
carving, sprigging; gas fired, cone 10
Photo by Molly Selznick

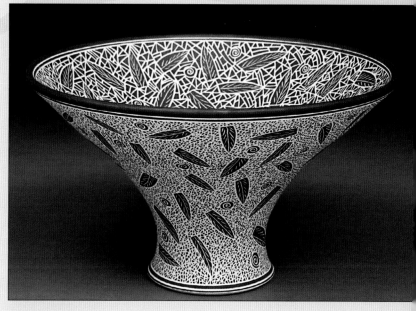

Becky Lloyd
Steve Lloyd
Bowl, 2008

9 x 10 x 10 inches (22.9 x 25.4 x 25.4 cm)
Wheel-thrown porcelain; brushed glaze; sgraf-
fito, terra sigilatta; electric fired, cone 10
Photo by artist

Matt Kelleher
Fry Pan Bowl, 2007

8 x 14 x 11 inches (20.3 x 35.6 x 27.9 cm)
Wheel-thrown stoneware; poured slip glaze; soda
fired, cone 10
Photo by artist

Becca Floyd
Stacked Bowls, 2008

2 x 6 x 3½ inches (30.5 x 15.2 x 8.9 cm)
Thrown and altered stoneware; brushed, sprayed,
dipped and stamped glaze; stamping;
gas fired in reduction, cone 10
Photo by Michael Davie

John Britt
Oil Spot Tea Bowl, 2008

6 x 4 x 4 inches (15.2 x 10.2 x 10.2 cm)
Wheel-thrown stoneware; dipped glaze; gas fired,
cone 11
Photo by artist

Becky Lloyd
Steve Lloyd
Plates, 2008

Largest: 2 x 10 x 10 inches (5 x 25.4 x 25.4 cm)
Wheel-thrown porcelain; brushed glaze; sgraffito, terra sigilatta;
electric fired, cone 10
Photo by artist

Shoko Teruyama
Cups, 2008

4½ x 4 x 4 inches (11.4 x 10.2 x 10.2 cm) each
Wheel-thrown earthenware; brushed glaze, sgraffito;
electric fired, cone 04
Photo by Matt Kelleher

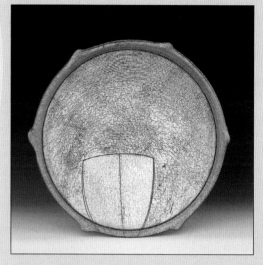

Lindsay Rogers
Plate, 2008

1½ x 11 x 11 inches (3.8 x 27.9 x 27.9 cm)
Wheel-thrown stoneware; porcelain slip, sgraffito,
oxide wash; wood/salt fired, cone 10
Photo by Marisa Falcigno

Kyle Carpenter
Plate, 2008

1½ x 9 x 9 inches (3.8 x 22.9 x 22.9 cm)
Wheel-thrown stoneware; poured flashing slip glaze; glaze brush-
work, underglaze brushwork; salt fired in gas kiln, cone 9
Photo by Tim Barnwell

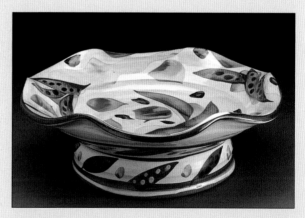

Stanley Mace Andersen
Pedestal Plate, 2005

3½ x 12 x 12 inches (8.9 x 30.5 x 30.5 cm)
Thrown and altered earthenware; dipped glaze;
maiolica technique; electric fired, cone 03
Photo by Tom Mills

Technique: **Throwing Off the Hump**

Throwing off the hump is a great way to throw several small pieces from one large lump of clay. You wedge only one piece of clay, and from it create multiple lids or spouts—or even tiny pots—that would otherwise be difficult to center effectively because they're made with such small amounts of clay.

■ LID DESIGNS

Take a look at the photo below. **1** There are two basic types of lids: *inset* (shown at left) and *overhanging* (shown at right). An inset lid fits inside a *galley*—a ledge that's thrown on the inside rim of the pot and that holds the lid in place. The lid on the Honey Pot project (see page 88) is an inset lid. An overhanging lid, on the other hand, is thrown with a *flange* on the underside of its rim. The lid of the Teapot project (see page 90) is this type. The throwing techniques are different for the two types of lids, and of course, each basic lid type has many variations. Structurally, certain lids are better suited for certain pots, but try whichever type appeals to your taste.

Try making a lid after you're confident in your ability to throw a centered pot. Achieving a good lid fit takes practice. I recommend making two lids for every pot you throw so that you can choose the better fitting one—and get some extra practice, too.

■ PREPARING TO THROW A LID

Make your pot first, keeping in mind if it will have an overhanging lid, the rim of the pot must be round and sturdy so that it won't chip when you remove and replace the lid. Using calipers, measure the diameter of the opening where the lid will fit—just inside the rim of the pot for overhanging lids **2** or from the inside corners of the galley for inset lids. **3** The most accurate measurements are taken from a freshly thrown pot. Remember, pots shrink as they dry!

> ▶ **Tip:** Calipers are used to measure the diameters of symmetrical forms. The double-ended ones work best for potters. One end records interior dimensions, and the other records exterior dimensions. Because these calipers are pivoted, no matter which end you use to record a dimension, the other end self-adjusts to that same dimension.

Now cone a large piece of clay—4 pounds (1.8 kg) should be enough for three or four small lids—and center the top portion only. The diameter of this centered section should be 1 inch (2.5 cm) narrower than the diameter of the pot's rim. From this point on, follow the instructions that are specific to the lid style you want to throw.

> ▶ **Tip:** When you want to make a lid larger than 5 inches (12.7 cm) in diameter, use the same forming techniques as for a smaller one, but throw it on a bat, not off the hump. Wide lids are too easy to distort when they're removed from the hump.

■ THROWING AN OVERHANGING LID

This lid style is thrown upside down. Start by sinking a hole in the centered portion of the clay. Then, using a claw-like grip, make a pull at the six o'clock position, as if you were throwing a bowl—but pull slightly upward and mostly outward. Compress the rim, keeping it at least ¾ inch (1.9 cm) thick. Depending on the size of lid you're making, continue making pulls (it doesn't take many), upward but mostly outward, while keeping the rim thick and compressed. **4**

With the wheel rotating slowly, split the rim of the lid in half to create a flange by applying inward pressure with your left thumb. **5** Check the diameter of the flange's outside edge, using the end of the calipers opposite to the end you used to measure the diameter of the opening in the pot. **6** If the lid doesn't quite measure up, press the flange inward with your thumb to decrease its diameter, or make it wider by pulling the flange outward, with your fingers inside.

With your eyes almost at the level of the lid, use a wooden modeling tool to cut a channel just below it. **7** Release the lid from the hump with a wire tool, being careful not to slice into the lid itself. To lift the lid off the hump without distorting it, pinch its thick base gently, using the thumbs and index fingers of both hands. **8** Place the lid on a ware board to dry; then invert and trim it (see Trimming a Lid on page 86).

■ THROWING AN INSET LID

Inset lids that aren't domed are thrown right side up. The lid in this demonstration sits slightly recessed in its pot and doesn't require trimming. Once it's leather hard, simply smooth its bottom edge with your thumb.

First you'll create a trough and a knob on the hump. At a point midway between the center of the clay and its outer edge, use your index and middle fingers to apply downward pressure. **9** Continue to refine the shape of the knob by compressing the clay with your fingertips. **10**

Pull the clay around the knob outward and slightly upward, using your left hand and a claw-like grip at the six o'clock position. Then flatten the rim by holding the flat edge of a metal rib to it. **11**

Measure the lid with the calipers. **12** Its outer rim should fit into the corner of the pot's galley. To adjust its diameter, either pull it outward, or trim away some clay with a needle tool.

Cut a groove with a wooden modeling tool, ¼ inch (6 mm) below the lid. Release the lid with a wire tool, and set it aside to dry.

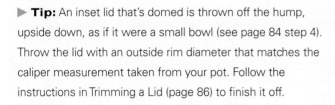

▶ **Tip:** An inset lid that's domed is thrown off the hump, upside down, as if it were a small bowl (see page 84 step 4). Throw the lid with an outside rim diameter that matches the caliper measurement taken from your pot. Follow the instructions in Trimming a Lid (page 86) to finish it off.

■ TRIMMING A LID

When both the lid and pot are leather hard, place the lid on the pot, and center the pot on the wheel. Affix the pot to the wheel head with three coils. Resting your left hand on the lid, trim the excess clay with a curved trimming tool. **13** Then smooth and compress it with a rubber rib. **14**

■ THROWING A SPOUT OFF THE HUMP

A spout can also be thrown off the hump. Its walls should be uniform, thickening only at the base, where the excess clay is used to attach it to a pot. Spouts tend to torque easily, so use light pressure when pulling the walls. Make several spouts so that you can select the one that best suits the pot.

Start with a 3- to 4-pound (1.4 to 1.8 kg) hump of clay. Each spout you throw should require less than 1 pound (.45 kg). Center the top of the hump so that it's 3 inches (7.6 cm) in diameter. Using two fingers, sink and then open a hole that's wider at the base of the spout than it is at the top. **15** Pull the walls up and in, first with a power pull and then with one regular pull. **16**

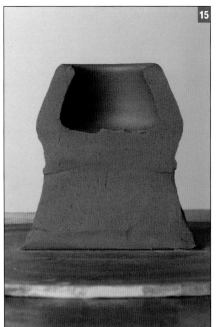

To taper the spout, grasp both its sides, about halfway down, so that it sits between the thumbs and index fingers of both hands. Gripping it gently, compress the clay inward as you lift up, easing the pressure as you reach the top. **17** This motion—*collaring*—narrows the opening but also makes the walls thicker, which can inhibit the flow of liquid. To avoid closing off the spout's opening completely, alternate between pulling and collaring. If the spout is too narrow for you to reach inside to make a pull, use a chopstick instead of a finger to support the inside of the wall. When you're finished, clean and smooth the spout with a metal rib, using gentle pressure.

To remove the spout from the hump, let the wheel rotate slowly as you ease a needle tool through it at the base. Hold your other hand nearby to catch the spout and lift it away. **18**

After 15 or 20 minutes, the spout will have set up a bit; it will still be flexible, but not as sticky. Support its sides with the thumb and index finger of one hand, and use the other hand to bend it by pulling down gently on its tip. **19** Allow the spout to dry to a soft leather-hard state before attaching it with slip to a leather-hard pot. (To see a similar spout on a finished pot, turn to page 90.)

Project: **Honey Pot**

This little pot is sweet enough to leave out on your kitchen table. You'll make it by throwing a cylinder form and giving it a belly for volume. With a galley thrown into the piece and an inset lid to match, this is a great project for any beginner eager to make his or her first lidded pot. Complete the piece by resting a honeycomb in its own special notches.

▲ **Tools**
Calipers, small knife

1 Center 2 pounds (.9 kg) of clay, and throw a cylinder. Compress the rim after each pull, and leave it about ½ inch (1.3 cm) thick.

2 Once the pot is about 5 inches (12.7 cm) tall, start making a galley by using your left thumbnail to split the thick rim gently. Continue applying downward pressure until the galley is finished.

RELATED TECHNIQUES

Centering	Throwing a Cylinder	Throwing Off the Hump (Inset Lid)	Decorating Surfaces
26	**29**	**85**	**68**

3 As you compress and smooth the walls of the pot between your hands and a metal rib, create the belly by pushing the middle of the wall outward, into the flexed edge of the rib.

▶ **Tip:** A weak galley chips easily. Start with a nice, thick rim, and don't overwork the galley by pressing it too far into the pot.

4 To make a matching lid, first use calipers to measure the diameter of the opening in the pot, from a corner of the galley to the corner opposite to it. Cut a channel at the base of the pot, release the pot with a wire tool, and transfer it to a ware board, being careful not to distort the rim. When the rim has stiffened to leather hard, invert the pot so that its base can dry, too.

5 Throw an inset lid off the hump to fit the diameter you registered with your calipers. When the pot and lid have dried to leather hard, roll and thumb both the bottom of the pot and the lid to smooth them. (Keep in mind that the lid will dry faster because it's smaller.)

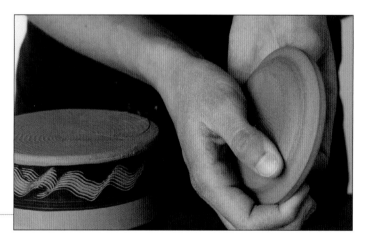

6 Use a small knife to cut a notch in both the lid and the galley for a honeycomb to rest in.

Black underglaze was applied in bands, and the sgraffito design was scratched through it with a serrated rib. After bisque firing, the entire piece was dipped in a clear glaze and fired again.

Project: **Teapot**

This teapot brings together all the skills you've learned so far. Entire books have been written about teapot mechanics, so be prepared: getting all the parts to work correctly *and* balance visually requires both focus and practice. The spout's position and shape are critical, and the handle must balance the weight of the full pot to create a visually harmonious whole.

⚠ **Tools**

Calipers, banding wheel (optional), serrated rib, long knife, chopstick, curved trimming tool, hole maker

RELATED TECHNIQUES

Centering	Throwing a Bowl	Trimming	Throwing Off the Hump	Pulling Handles	Decorating Surfaces (Slip Trailing)
26	**54**	**58**	**82**	**35**	**70**

1 Center 4 pounds (1.8 kg) of clay on a bat. Sink a hole, leaving enough clay at the bottom to allow for trimming a foot ring later. Using a claw-like grip at the six o'clock position, lift the clay upward and slightly outward with your left hand, as if you were pulling a deep bowl.

2 With the next pull, you'll create the continuous curve on the inside. Begin by pulling as you would for a bowl, working the clay upward and outward, but halfway through this pull, allow your outside (right) hand to apply the dominant pressure so that you're pulling the clay upward and *inward*.

3 Once you've established the wall thickness and height (leave the base thick to allow for a foot ring and to support the belly of the pot), refine the curves of your teapot by compressing the walls between your hand and a metal rib.

4 Compress the rim and smooth it with a chamois. Measure the diameter inside the rim with calipers, then throw an overhanging lid, off the hump, to fit the rim. When the rims of the pot and lid have stiffened, invert them so that the bottoms can dry to leather hard.

▶ **Tip:** The rim of a teapot should be wide enough to allow the pot to be cleaned, but if it's too wide, liquid may leak from under the lid before it can exit through the spout.

5 While the pot and lid are drying, throw a spout off the hump. (You may use the same hump of clay that you used for the lid.) Be sure to taper its tip; a flared tip will spew tea rather than pour it in a stream (figure 6). Allow the spout to set up for 15 to 20 minutes. Then bend its tip to curve it (see page 87), and allow it to dry.

A flared spout spews tea.   A tapered spout pours properly.

Figure 6

6 When the lid is leather hard, place it on the pot. Center the pot on the wheel and affix it with three coils of clay. With a curved trimming tool in your right hand and your left hand resting on the lid, trim away the excess clay. Then, as the wheel continues to rotate, smooth and compress the lid with a rubber rib.

▶ **Tip:** Be careful not to allow the spout to dry faster than the pot itself; they should both be leather hard when you attach them. If the spout begins to reach the leather-hard stage before the pot does, cover it with plastic to prevent it from drying too much. Spritz it lightly with water if it becomes leather hard too soon.

7 Remove the lid, invert the pot, and affix it to the wheel with coils. Using a trimming tool, trim it to create a foot ring at the base of the pot. While it's still upside down, refine the curve at its base, and compress this area with a rubber rib.

If the tip of the spout is too low, tea pours before the pot is full. Correct spout placement allows the pot to be filled.

Figure 7

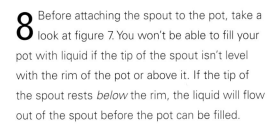

8 Before attaching the spout to the pot, take a look at figure 7. You won't be able to fill your pot with liquid if the tip of the spout isn't level with the rim of the pot or above it. If the tip of the spout rests *below* the rim, the liquid will flow out of the spout before the pot can be filled.

9 Place the leather-hard pot on a banding wheel or on any elevated surface that's at eye level, and hold the spout behind the pot so that you can view their profiles in relation to one another. As you move the spout's position to a height and angle that suit you, keep the following facts in mind. The spout should curve outward, not upward; it should resemble a pointing finger rather than a beckoning one. Its height on the pot is important, too. When you've found a placement that meets these requirements and that pleases you, use a chopstick to trace the profile of the pot onto the wide end of the spout.

10 Using a long knife, cut along the traced line on the spout so that it will attach to the pot at an angle.

11 Hold the spout against the pot in the position you've chosen for it, and trace a line around it onto the pot.

12 Use a hole maker to pierce several holes through the pot, within the traced line for the spout, keeping them at least ¼ inch (6 mm) inside the traced line and spacing them in an even pattern.

13 Using a serrated rib, score the areas on the spout and the pot where the two will be joined; then apply slip to these areas. Gently press the spout onto the pot, checking all around it to be sure it's attached well and isn't crooked. Use your thumb to press and smooth the clay around its outer edges.

14 Pull a handle for your teapot, holding the pot by its foot and tilting it at an angle. Score and slip to attach the handle opposite to the spout. The handle must balance the weight of the pot when it's full, and must also be visually balanced relative to the other parts of the pot. Generally, a handle placed toward the top half of the pot will make serving easier.

After the handle was attached, dots of thick slip were applied with a slip-trailing bulb. The teapot was then bisque fired and dipped in a transparent blue glaze. A brush was used to apply dabs of a runny blue glaze over the dots, and the piece was fired again.

Project: **Tulipiere**

This creative flower holder is a great alternative to a regular vase for artfully displaying your favorite blooms. In this project, you'll learn to throw a closed form, with a pierced pattern and a cut lid. The tulipiere is altered slightly to create lobes that lend it a full, yet soft quality.

⚠ **Tools**
Large wooden rib, ceramic chuck and towel, banding wheel (optional), thick slip, slip-trailing bulb, chopstick, small knife

1 Center 3 pounds (1.4 kg) of clay and throw a cylinder, pulling the walls upward and inward so the form tapers at the top. Stop making pulls before the walls get thin.

▶ **Tip:** A piece of foam will work in place of the chuck and towel (see step 7), but for instructions on making your own ceramic chucks, see page 119. To mix the thick slip required for this project, refer to page 120.

2 Beginning about one-third of the way down the side of your pot, make a chocking motion by approaching the pot with both hands, one at the nine o'clock position and the other at the three o'clock position. Gently compress the pot's walls between both hands to work them inward. (This technique is known as *collaring*.) Raise your hands as you compress to the top of the pot.

3 Make a regular pull, beginning about halfway down the pot, and pull upward and inward as much as possible.

4 Continue alternating between pulling and collaring. Then collar the opening completely closed, trapping air inside your piece. As the wheel rotates, pinch any remaining clay in your fingertips until it detaches.

5 Using a metal rib, clean and smooth the exterior. Notice how the air that's trapped inside the form resists the pressure you apply.

6 Now it's time to shape the lobes of your tulipiere. Stop the wheel. Gently press one end of a large wooden rib into the base, and rock the rib's edge all the way up the wall to indent the clay. Make the next indentation directly opposite to the first one. Repeat to divide the surface of the pot into eight lobes. Release the pot from the wheel head, and allow it to stiffen.

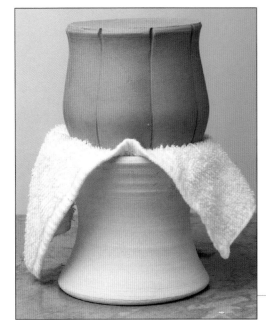

7 Set the stiffened tulipiere upside down on a chuck, with a towel in between to protect your pot. (If you don't have a chuck, just rest the form on its side, on a piece of foam.) Allow the base to get leather hard.

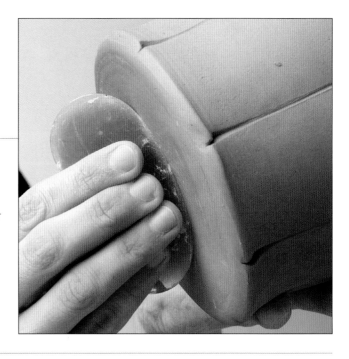

8 Once the piece is leather hard, roll its bottom edge on the table, and thumb it smooth. Then use a rubber rib to smooth the very bottom, and to press the bottom inward just a bit to make it slightly concave.

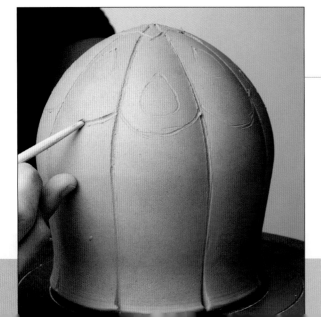

9 Place your tulipiere on a banding wheel or another elevated surface. Using a chopstick or dull pencil, draw staggered teardrop shapes on the lobes and a simple petal shape at the very top. You'll cut the lid of this tulipiere from the piece itself. To help guide you as you make this cut, draw a scalloped guideline around the entire piece, following the curves of the lobes.

10 To make the teardrop-shaped holes, poke the blade of a small knife through the clay, and cut along the lines. You'll find that cutting these shapes out is a lot like carving a pumpkin. Also cut out the petal-shaped hole in the top.

11 To cut out the lid, insert the knife at a 45° angle, and carefully cut along the marked line, keeping the tool angled. (The angle will prevent the lid from sliding off the pot.) Gently lift the lid off the pot, being careful not to distort it, and then replace it to dry while it's on the pot. When the lid has reached the hard leather-hard stage, smooth any rough edges if necessary.

12 The lid will fit correctly on the pot in only one position. To help identify that position, make a *key* by using a slip-trailing bulb to apply two dots of thick slip—one on the pot and another just above it on the lid.

The bisque-fired tulipiere was dipped in a matte green glaze and fired again.

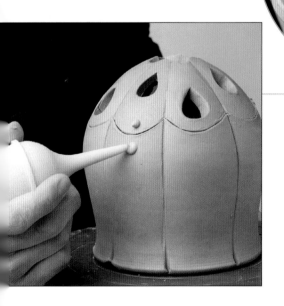

Gallery:
Lidded Vessels

Scott Cornish
Teapot, 2008

5 x 8 x 5 inches (12.7 x 20.3 x 12.7 cm)
Thrown and altered porcelain; natural ash glaze;
wood fired, cone 12
Photo by artist

Becca Floyd
Covered Jar with Tray, 2008

15 x 8 x 13 inches (38.1 x 20.3 x 33 cm)
Wheel-thrown stoneware; sprayed, dipped, and
stamped glaze; stamping, oxide wash; gas fired in
reduction, cone 10
Photo by artist

Kelly O'Briant
Fancy Bloom Canister Set, 2008

Largest: 11 x 7 inches (27.9 x 17.8 cm)
Wheel-thrown and trimmed porcelain;
dipped glaze; underglaze brushwork,
overglaze; electric fired, cone 6
Photo by Tom Mills

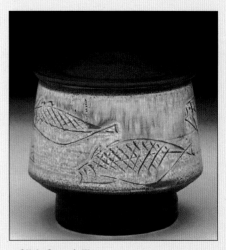

Silvie Granatelli
Fish Jar, 2008

5 x 4 x 4 inches (12.7 x 10.2 x 10.2 cm)
Wheel-thrown porcelain; dipped glaze;
carving; gas fired, cone 10
Photo by Molly Selznick

Becky Lloyd
Steve Lloyd
Lidded Jar, 2008

14 x 9 x 9 inches (35.6 x 22.9 x 22.9 cm)
Wheel-thrown porcelain; brushed glaze; sgraffito,
terra sigilatta; electric fired, cone 10
Photo by artist

Joey Sheehan
Teapot, 2008

6 x 8 inches (15.2 x 20.3 cm)
Wheel-thrown stoneware; sprayed glaze; slip trail-
ing; gas fired in reduction, cone 10
Photo by Steve Mann

Benjamin Carter
Teapot Stack, 2007

14 x 14 x 14 inches (35.6 x 35.6 x 35.6 cm)
Wheel-thrown porcelain; dipped glaze; residual
soda; soda fired in gas kiln in reduction, cone 10
Photo by artist

Ellen Shankin
Soup Tureen, 1994

9 x 14 x 14 inches (22.9 x 35.6 x 35.6 cm)
Wheel-thrown stoneware; sprayed and dipped glaze;
gas fired, cone 9
Photo by Tim Barnwell

Matt Kelleher
Teapot, 2008

6 x 7 x 6 inches (15.2 x 17.8 x 15.2 cm)
Wheel-thrown stoneware; poured slip glaze;
soda fired, cone 10
Photo by artist

Stanley Mace Andersen
Coffee Server with Demitasse, 2007

9½ x 8½ x 4½ inches (24.1 x 21.6 x 11.4 cm)
Wheel-thrown earthenware; dipped glaze;
maiolica technique; cone 03
Photo by Tom Mills

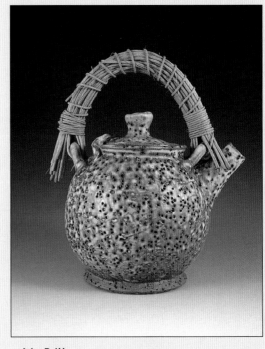

John Britt
Tea Ball Tea, 2007

10 x 8 x 8 inches (25.4 x 20.3 x 20.3 cm)
Wheel-thrown stoneware; dipped glaze;
cane handle; gas fired, cone 10
Photo by artist

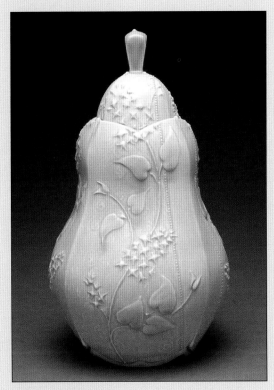

Bradley C. Birkhimer
Chinese Red Teapot, 2008

6 x 8½ x 4 inches (15.2 x 21.6 x 10.2 cm)
Wheel-thrown porcelaneous stoneware; dipped
glaze; wood fired with salt and soda, cone 11
Photo by artist

Kristen Kieffer
Pear Covered Jar, Lilacs, 2008

14 x 8 x 8 inches (35.6 x 20.3 x 20.3 cm)
Thrown and altered porcelain; brushed and dipped
glaze; carving, slip trailing; electric fired, cone 7
Photo by artist

Leah Leitson
Tea Set, 2006

Teapot: 9 x 7 x 5½ inches (22.9 x 17.8 x 14 cm)
Wheel-thrown porcelain; sprayed glaze; applied clay;
electric fired, cone 6
Photo by Tim Barnwell

A Brief Overview of Firing

The firing process that turns clay into durable, functional objects takes place in a kiln. Although a kiln is superficially similar to a household oven, you don't just set its temperature, pop in a pot, and walk away. The ceramic firing process requires you to load the kiln carefully with ware and then bring it to the appropriate maturing temperature in controlled stages. You may sacrifice a few of your pots to the Kiln God at first, but with a little time, attention, and practice, you'll learn how to achieve desirable results.

MOST FUNCTIONAL CLAY WORK IS FIRED TWICE. The first—or bisque—firing makes the clay hard and porous, and readies it for an application of glaze. The second—or glaze—firing, at a higher, maturing temperature, melts the glaze and seals it to the surface of the pot. For a refresher about clay bodies and firing temperatures, see pages 8–9.

SELECTING A KILN

When you're ready to invest in a kiln, I recommend starting with an electric one; it's easy to operate and yields predictable results. Some electric kilns can be operated manually; others include a computerized control system. You'll need a proper power supply and a well-ventilated area for an electric kiln; outdoors and under cover—where the risk of fumes and fire is minimized—is the ideal setting. You can use an electric kiln indoors, but you must have a vent system and place the kiln well away from walls and flammable objects.

Large, hand-built, gas-fueled, and outdoor wood-fired kilns are used to achieve unique results by controlling the kiln's *atmosphere* (the amount of oxygen present in the kiln during firing; see Kiln Atmospheres on page 109). These kilns are complex pieces of equipment; consider one for your studio only after you've trained with an experienced potter.

PYROMETRIC CONES

To monitor the progress of the firing, potters use *pyrometric cones*, which are made of a blend of ceramic materials that melt when they reach a specific temperature. Think of cones as similar to single-use thermometers. Set inside the kiln at the start of the firing, they measure the *heat work*—the temperature rise per hour. You peek

This used cone pack is from a kiln that was fired to cone 10.

through a *peephole* in the kiln (a small opening that allows you to see inside) to watch their progress as they react to the heat; as the temperature climbs, their tips begin to arc over. When a cone's tip reaches the level of its base, the target temperature and rate of temperature rise have been attained, and it's time to start the kiln-cooling process.

Different cones are made to monitor every possible kiln temperature to which potters might want to fire their work. They're assigned numbers that represent the temperatures at which they melt, from 022—a cone that melts at a very low temperature—right up through 01, 1, 2, and beyond, which melt at increasingly higher temperatures. See the chart at right.

Cone-Firing Ranges

Cone	Range
022...04	Low-fire (earthenware)
03	
02	
01	
1	
2	
3	
4	Mid-range (stoneware)
5	
6	
7	
8	High-fire (stoneware)
9	
10	
11	
12	

To support cones, you make a *cone pack*. Roll a ½-inch-wide (1.3 cm) coil of clay, and press your thumb into one end to create a reservoir for catching the melted cones. Press the wide ends of the three cones into the coil: a *target cone* that's rated to your desired temperature; a cone rated one number lower, a *guide* cone; and another rated one number higher, a *guard* cone. Then pinch the clay at their bases to hold them in place. Make sure that the numbers on the cones are all facing in the same direction.Let the cone pack dry thoroughly before placing it in the kiln.

Line the three cones up sequentially in the cone pack, beginning with the lowest-rated one.

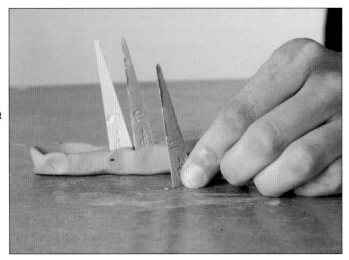

Cones are made to stand at a slight angle; make sure to set them in the cone pack at that same angle.

If your kiln doesn't have a *pyrometer* (a temperature-reading device), you'll rely completely on cones; however, some electric kilns come with pyrometers. This device is either connected to a computer with a digital screen that displays the kiln temperature, or has prongs that hold a small cone specifically sized to fit them. When this cone melts, the pyrometer automatically turns off the kiln. Should the kiln malfunction, a cone pack in it could save the day, so always use one, even if your kiln is completely automatic. Position the cone pack on a kiln shelf that is level with a peephole, and confirm that the pack is visible from the outside.

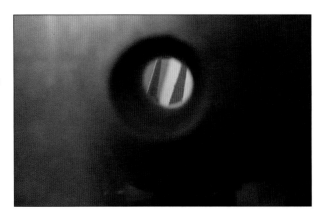

The peepholes built into the sides of electric kilns allow you to monitor the progress of the firing.

▓ LOADING THE KILN

Kiln shelves and *kiln furniture* (stilts in various sizes) hold your pots in place during firing.

The kiln shelves that your ware rests on must be protected from glaze drips with a coating of *kiln wash* (a liquid mixture of refractory materials). The brushed-on layers of wash allow you to chip off glaze drips easily, without damaging the shelf.

Here's a kiln wash recipe:

Mix 50 percent EPK (Edgar Plastic Kaolin) and 50 percent alumina hydrate with water to the consistency of whole milk. (Remember to put on your respirator before handling these powdered materials!) Apply two to three coats of the wash with a brush, letting it dry to the touch between each application.

An assortment of kiln shelves and stilts in different lengths makes it easier to load ware into your kiln efficiently.

Use kiln wash as a protective coating for your kiln shelves.

Whenever possible, always fire full kiln loads. Placing as many pots as will fit comfortably inside the kiln helps save energy and reduces uneven heating. Ideally, a load contains pots of various sizes. For a space- and heat-efficient load, place pots of similar heights on the same shelf. Small pieces fit nicely between large and/or wide ones. The best place for tall pieces is on the top shelf; tall pots placed on lower shelves can make the stacks wobbly. Stack the shelves on stilts, and to keep the shelves from warping or cracking over time, always place the stilts in the same positions on them. For optimum heat distribution,

Three stilts support each of the staggered shelves in this kiln.

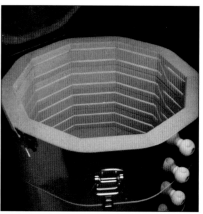

The glowing elements of a firing electric kiln
Photo used with permission from Skutt Kilns.

stagger the shelf heights, and leave about ½-inch (1.3 cm) of space between the tops of the pots and the kiln shelf above, as well as between any pots and the *thermocouple* (the heat-sensitive probe in the kiln that's connected to the pyrometer).

For space-efficiency during bisque firings, you can load pots so that they touch each other and stack them on top of one another, as well. Make sure that stacked pieces nest well, though; don't place them directly on the rims of the pots underneath them. The rims of greenware are fragile and can crack. The stress created by stacking more than three pots on top of one another can also crack the bottom piece.

When loading for a glaze firing, place pots at least ¼ inch (6 mm) away from one another, and from stilts and the kiln shelf above. A glazed pot will stick to anything it touches! Also make sure that the bottoms of your pieces are free of glaze. Glaze on the inside of a foot ring is fine, but the bottom of

The bowls on the left are incorrectly stacked; the rim of the bowl on the bottom is likely to crack from the weight of the one on top. Correctly stacked pieces appear on the right: note how their feet are aligned.

the foot, which contacts the kiln shelf, should be left unglazed. Since pots in glaze firings can't touch, fewer pieces fit into the kiln than in a bisque firing.

Once your kiln is loaded, position your cones, and close the kiln lid. Electric kilns can be fired according to the manufacturer's recommended schedule. Fire is always a risk with kilns but is easy to avoid if you take the recommended safety precautions. Even automatic kilns can malfunction, so monitor the kiln regularly and make sure to confirm that it shuts off properly.

THE FIRING PROCESS

Whether your kiln requires only the simple press of a button or continuous monitoring and adjusting, it's important to have a basic understanding of the physical and chemical changes that happen to the pottery inside it during firing.

From the time the kiln is turned on until it reaches about 430°F (221°C), any remaining physical water is driven out of the clay. If the greenware you've loaded is damp, the temperature should be held at 212°F (100°C)—the boiling point of water—to allow moisture to escape; rapid heating can cause clay to explode as water turns into steam. From that point, the temperature should climb gradually; organic matter and chemical water will burn out of the clay body during this period, as the body changes physically to become ceramic.

These two unglazed pieces were made using the same clay body, but the one on the left was fired in an oxidation atmosphere and the one on the right in a reduction atmosphere.

During the process of glaze firing, minerals in the clay flux and vitrify (see page 8). The temperature range at which vitrification takes place depends on the mineral content of the clay body you're firing. As a glaze reaches its maturation temperature, it becomes viscous, melts fully, and bonds to the pot. After the firing, the kiln must cool slowly so the glaze can reach its *set point* (the point at which a glaze cools and hardens), and then later, so that *thermal shock* doesn't take place. (If ceramic wares are cooled too quickly, they can crack from the shock.) When the desired temperature is reached, the kiln is shut off and left to cool. Cooling can take from several hours to several days, depending on the kiln and how well it's insulated. Before opening the kiln, wait until its temperature is below 200°F (93°C) or until a piece of paper held in front of a peephole doesn't turn brown from heat.

Just as throwing pots takes practice, so does firing them. I recommend training with an experienced kiln firer if you have the opportunity. Ask questions and keep notes so you can track any adjustments you've made during different firings, and record your results. A written record is invaluable for future firings.

▓ KILN ATMOSPHERES

The proportion of oxygen to fuel inside a kiln creates its *atmosphere*. The atmospheric conditions during the firing create chemical changes, both in the clay and glaze, which affect their color, opacity, and texture. And, to make things even more interesting, the atmosphere can fluctuate and change throughout a firing. In the (usually) tightly controlled environment of an electric kiln, an excess of oxygen is present, producing an *oxidation atmosphere*. In a *neutral atmosphere*, the balance between available oxygen and energy is perfect and efficient. Like oxidation atmospheres, neutral atmospheres generally yield bright colors. In a *reduction atmosphere*, there's less oxygen than fuel, so the fuel isn't completely combusted. Reduction can be achieved in fuel-fired gas, oil, or wood kilns because the air-to-fuel ratio can be adjusted during the firing. Reduction produces a wide range of glaze variations.

When you purchase commercial glazes (see page 111), keep in mind that the samples you're likely to see, with their bright, clean colors, have been fired in the oxidation atmosphere of an electric kiln. Your results are likely to be somewhat different because no two kilns seem to be exactly alike. When you're mixing your own glazes, there's more to consider. You can adjust proportions of ingredients or make informed substitutions to achieve different effects. Regardless of whether you use premixed commercial glazes or mix your own, if you're careful to take notes and get plenty of firing practice, you'll learn how to recognize and control the variables to get the results you want.

By now, you understand that the process of making pottery takes time and practice. Within the many steps required—from throwing a pot to firing a kiln full of glazed pieces—are endless avenues for exploration and creativity. Some basic information, paired with the desire to create and experiment, will ensure many years of pottery-making enjoyment.

Glaze Fundamentals

An enjoyable part of this next phase of making pots is discovering the art and science of glazing. Perhaps you've thrown enough pots now to have fired a bisque load. Once you have, they're ready for the glaze coat. Properly applied and then fired, a vitreous glaze can add an entirely new dimension to your hard-won work.

A pot's glaze may be transparent or opaque, matte or glossy. Its color can be flat or variegated, runny-looking or stiff. Whatever the final result, all glazes contain three basic materials: *silica* (a glass former) fuses the glaze to the clay; *flux* makes the glaze melt (various minerals can do this); and a *stabilizer*, usually made from some form of clay, keeps the glaze from melting too much and running off the pot. Oxides, carbonates, or stains are added to glaze formulations to produce color, transparency, opacity, and texture. Keep your glazes out of freezing temperatures, and store them in sealed containers.

Glazes consist of dry, powdered materials mixed with water.

These test tiles show a variety of glaze characteristics on different clay bodies. From top to bottom: runny, opaque, stiff, matte, glossy, and transparent

During firing, the glaze interacts with the clay and, of course, with the heat itself—melting, changing, and fusing permanently to the surface. Your pot is at stake, so matching your glaze's firing range to that of the clay you've thrown is important. Make sure that your clay body and glaze are *compatible*—that is, that the two are capable of withstanding the same firing temperature—and that you know the temperature to which your glaze should be fired. Glaze made for low-fire pottery fails at high-fire temperatures; it will melt and damage your kiln and equipment. On the other hand, a glaze that is under-fired won't mature or be food safe.

Commercial glazes in different quantities are available from ceramic suppliers in ready-to-use liquid form. Unfortunately, these commonly come in small containers; they don't last long, and they limit the application methods you can use. The best choices for beginners are commercial glazes that come premixed in a dry, powdered form; you simply add water and then sieve the mixture. It's easy to mix these up in large quantities that will last a long time and that also make their application easy. And the only special tool you need is a sieve for smoothing the glaze once you've mixed it with water. Be sure to read the labels on these glazes—and their instructions for proper use. Not all glazes are food-safe; the ones that are will say so. Most beginners start off using commercial glazes; they're easy to acquire, so you can gain practice with your application techniques.

The most cost-effective option is to purchase individual, dry materials in bulk and, following a specific glaze recipe, weigh out quantities of each one, add water, and sieve the mixture to smooth it. (For instructions on making your own glazes from scratch, see Recipes on page 123.) This method works well for potters who want to develop their own, unique glaze palettes, but beginners should first receive some training from an experienced

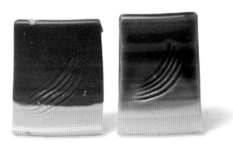

These two test tiles have the same glaze on them. The tile on the right was fired to maturity, but the one on the left was under-fired: the glaze didn't melt completely and is rough, not glassy.

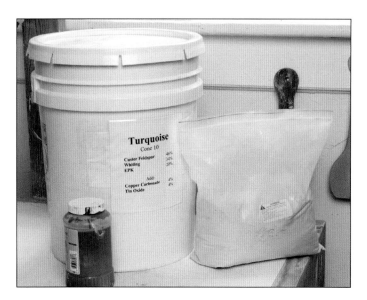

Left to right: **A bottle of liquid commercial glaze, a labeled bucket of glaze made from scratch, and a bag of commercial, premixed dry glaze**

The low-fire product on the test tile at the right mimics the textural effect of the high-fire glaze on the tile at the left.
Photo used with permission from AMACO.

potter. Making your own glazes from raw materials requires a significant investment in additional safety and mixing equipment, materials, storage space, and time.

A range of bright glaze colors is possible with low-fire earthenware clay bodies. Higher firing temperatures limit the range of glaze colors somewhat, as some of the raw materials that yield brighter colors burn out during firing. (Remember: under-firing isn't a good idea.) The captions that accompany the photographs at the end of each project in this book provide general information about the glazes I used. In some cases, I used high-fire materials, but you should be able to achieve similar effects with commercial low- or mid-range glazes.

Most of the glaze recipes in this book (see Recipes on page 122) can be applied by using the techniques described in the next chapter. Do keep notes about your glazes. Make a small sketch of your pot, and write down the glaze you used next to it, as well as the results. That way, you'll have a record of which glaze combinations you like best.

Just as there's no single "right" form for a pot, there's no "right" glaze. The many variables of the glazing process provide endless avenues of investigation. The dishes pictured at right, for example, are similar in size and form, but have been treated with different glaze combinations. Try making a series of identical pots, using different glazes on each of them and firing them all together in the same kiln. Then ask yourself which one or ones are successful and why. Make notes in your

Emily Reason
Flower Dishes, 2007

Various sizes
Porcelain; cone 10, reduction fired
Photo by Mary Vogel

sketchbook to help you understand how the different results were produced. The clay body color, your glaze application method, the kiln atmosphere, and the firing temperature all have various effects on finished pieces. Treat your first pots as educational experiments with the many aspects of glazing and firing. They're fun and informative processes! And if you're both careful and adventurous, they'll always be fascinating.

Technique: **Applying Glazes**

The process of making pottery takes a dramatic shift at the glazing stage. As you face the challenge of how to glaze the surface in a way that will flatter the form, keep in mind that even simple glazing can be very expressive. You only need a few glazes (and application methods) to be able to create interesting combinations.

Sometimes a single glaze is enough. Occasionally, you may want to line the interior of a pot with one glaze and the exterior with a contrasting color. Layered glazes can lend visual depth to the surfaces of your pots. If your pot has a surface texture or sgraffito work, choose a glaze that will complement it, such as a transparent or semitransparent glaze that won't mask all that carefully created detail.

Usually, you'll want to fire your pieces shortly after you've glazed them. If firing must be delayed, that's fine; just cover your pots with a clean plastic sheet to keep them free of dust. Glaze that's been applied to a pot is fragile, so handle the pot carefully. If the glaze chips, simply dab more on that area with a brush before firing.

■ BASIC GLAZING TOOLS

Basic glazing tools include brushes with soft, full bristles; a foam brush; a sponge; a banding wheel; and a bucket of clean water (see page 16-21). Depending on the application technique you use, you'll also want to have on hand the items shown at right.

Clockwise from top: Jug of wax resist, drill with paint-mixing attachment, dipping tongs, and a liquid measuring cup

■ PREPARING TO GLAZE

To prepare your pieces for glazing, first use a damp sponge to clean off any dust from the surface of your bisque-fired pot. (The sponge shouldn't be soaking wet; glaze won't adhere properly to saturated bisqueware.) Bits of dust or dirt—even oil from your hands—can disrupt the glaze's performance and cause defects. **1**

The bottoms of your pieces or other areas that might come in contact with the kiln shelf must be free of glaze; if they're not, when the glaze melts, the pots will fuse to the shelf. Wax resist can be handy here, as it repels glaze from any areas to which it's applied. Some resists are sold ready to use; others need diluting, so read the labels for instructions. On a pot with a tall foot, just apply the resist to the very bottom of the foot ring, since this area is the only one that will contact the kiln shelf. It's also a good idea to wax at least ¼ inch (6 mm) up the side of the pot in case the glaze is runny.

Dip a foam brush into the resist, scrape the excess wax from the brush on the side of the container so the wax won't drip, and brush it onto the pot. **2** (The easiest way to remove accidental wax drips from a bisque-fired pot is to bisque fire the pot again.) Set the waxed pieces on their rims to dry completely; this usually takes about 30 minutes. **3** If the wax feels sticky, it's not quite dry yet.

Glazes tend to settle over time, so stir yours well before you begin, using the stirring utensil to lift and mix in the material that's settled on the bottom, until the glaze is free of lumps. Re-stir it every few minutes while you're glazing.

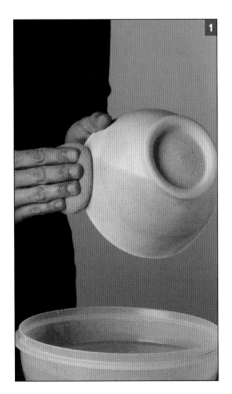

> ▶ **Tip:** Use clean utensils for mixing and clean containers for storing them. Cross-contamination can ruin a glaze, so always rinse your stirrer or brush before using it in another glaze. And *always* wash your hands after glazing and before eating.

■ APPLICATION TECHNIQUES

Different glaze-application techniques can enhance the surface of your pottery in different ways. But remember: the final appearance of the glaze you use will be influenced by a number of factors, including the color of your clay. Also keep in mind that the glazes in commercial glaze catalogs are shown as they would look when fired on a white clay body.

Following are a few tips that will help you achieve successful glaze effects:

No matter which glazing method you use, the best glaze application is even in thickness. Usually, a single coat is sufficient. As a general rule of thumb, a glaze coat should be about as thick as a dime.

Most glazes dry before your very eyes, but be sure not to touch a piece until the glaze no longer reflects light—the best indication that it's dry. The glazed mug shown on the right-hand side of the photo at the top is still wet; you can see the telltale light reflection on its rim. **4**

When you've finished glazing a piece, always check its bottom for beads of glaze. Wipe these off, or they'll fuse your pot to the kiln shelf during firing. **5** Should you make a mistake while glazing, you can wash the glaze off with a sponge and running water, but let the pot dry for a couple of days before glazing it again. Glaze won't stick to saturated bisqueware.

Dipping

Dipping—submerging a piece in a bucket of glaze—is the quickest and easiest application method, and also ensures an even application. You'll need a bucket of glaze that's large enough to dip the piece you've made. Small pieces, such as cups and small bowls, fit into a 1-gallon

(3.8 L) bucket of glaze; larger pieces may require one that holds 5 gallons (19 L).

To glaze an entire piece all at once, use dipping tongs to hold it while you submerge it in the glaze bucket. Grip the pot securely with the tongs, but not too firmly, and hold it at an angle so that as you lower it into the bucket, it fills with glaze. **6** Submerge the entire pot, count to three, and then slowly lift it out and turn it upside down to pour off the

excess glaze. **7** Use a brush to touch up the marks left by the tongs. **8**

To glaze only the exterior of a pot, turn it upside down, grip its foot, and dip it straight down into the glaze. **9** Keeping the rim of the pot level with the surface of the glaze creates an air pocket inside so that glaze won't enter the pot's interior. Hold the piece in the glaze to a count of three. Then gently pull your pot straight up and out of the glaze, and allow the excess to drip off.

Pouring

Pouring works well for glazing the interiors of pots and on large pieces, and can even be used as a decorative technique. You don't need a large bucket of glaze for pouring, but you do need to pour carefully and try not to splash.

▶ **Tip:** When you plan to glaze both the interior and exterior of a pot, it's best to apply glaze to the interior first so that if you splash any on the outer surface, it won't disrupt a glaze that's already there. Accidental spills on the unglazed exterior can be wiped off with a damp sponge.

Hold your pot at an angle over the glaze bucket, and pour the glaze slowly into your pot to prevent splashing. **10** (Using a liquid measuring cup with a lip designed for pouring is helpful.) Fill about half of the pot with glaze; then tip it upright and roll the glaze around carefully so that it coats the interior, right up to just below the rim. Now, while holding the pot over the bucket, slowly pour out the excess glaze,

rotating the pot as you do. **11**

Pieces that are too large or wide to be dipped may also be glazed by pouring. Find a large plastic container that's bigger than your pot, set two flat sticks across it, and rest the pot on the sticks. Scoop glaze up with a cup and gradually pour it over the piece, allowing the excess to drip into the container beneath. **12** The glaze that drips off can be returned to the original glaze container when you're finished.

For decorative effects, you can pour additional glaze onto small areas of a piece that's already coated with a base coat. With one hand, hold your pot at an angle over the glaze bucket or another container. With the other hand, scoop up some glaze in a small container. (A spoon works well for very small amounts.) Bring the container into contact with your pot; then slowly pour the glaze from it, allowing the glaze to drip down the piece and into the large container beneath. **13** I glazed the Plate project on page 62 by layering colored glazes over a speckled white base glaze.

Layered Glazes

The elegant, sweeping lines of simple brushwork add a painterly quality to the surface of your work. An animal-hair brush with long bristles works well because it holds a lot of glaze. To get a feel for how to hold and manipulate brushes of all sizes, practice with them using India ink on newsprint. **14** Also try different ways of making brush strokes to create various qualities of line, by using the side of a brush or just its tip, for example. To make full strokes, use your entire arm rather than your wrist or fingers.

When applying glaze on top of a base coat, you'll have to experiment to find out how the two will interact. Stiff glazes that don't move or run in the firing are best for retaining a brushed design.

When you do brushwork on pottery, make sure you're comfortable. Either hold your pot or place it on a banding wheel at eye level. Dip the brush into the glaze to load it up, and scrape the excess off on the edge of the glaze container.

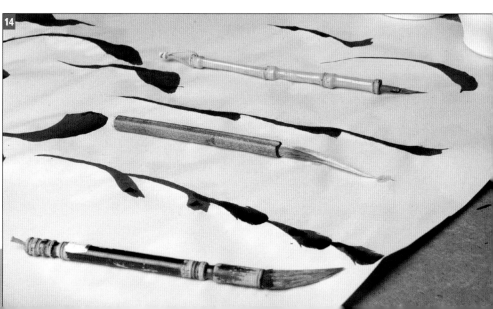

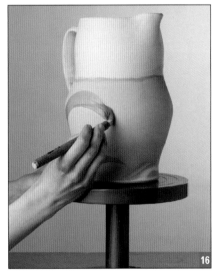

Underglaze is an excellent brushwork medium. For the best application, brush it onto pots at the leather-hard or bone-dry stage, before bisque firing. **15** You may also apply underglaze to bisqueware, but you run the risk of smudging your design when you apply glaze on top of it. To avoid this problem, bisque fire the piece again after applying the underglaze, and then apply the glaze. Unlike many glazes, fired underglazes are generally the same colors as they are in the bottle; however, the thickness of the application and the glaze that you place on top will affect the results. Some underglaze colors require the application of more than one coat; read the label for instructions specific to the one you're using.

Glaze layering with wax resist is a simple technique that yields impressive results. First, a coat of glaze is applied to the entire piece. When the glaze is dry, a pattern is brushed on in wax, and then the piece is dipped into a second glaze. In the finished piece, the bottom glaze layer shines through the brushed-on pattern.

Start by applying the glaze base coat. When the base coat is dry, use a brush to apply the wax resist. To make a spiral pattern, choose a long, thin brush. Begin your mark with the tip, and lay the bristles on the pot as you swirl your stroke around. **16** Allow the wax to dry completely; if it isn't completely dry, it won't resist the top layer of glaze as it should. Then dip the pot into the

glaze you've chosen for your top layer. When you lift the pot out, notice how the glaze pulls away from the waxed areas. **17**

Layering glazes certainly creates interesting effects. For endlessly surprising results, combine two or more methods, such as dipping the entire piece in a base coat, then doing simple brushwork on top with one or two different glazes. Another simple layering method involves dipping half of a pot in one glaze and the other half in another, and allowing the two to overlap a bit. **18** No matter what experiments you choose to make, when you layer glazes, always make sure that the bottom layer is dry before applying another glaze on top.

Technique: **Handy and Homemade**

Some of the tools that a potter needs are easy to make and less expensive than the commercial versions, including foam bats, chucks, and stamps. If you happen to have some woodcutting and sanding tools, there's no limit to the inventive, custom tools you can create. You may not need any of these handmade items right away, but the instructions that follow will help you make a few when you're ready.

■ FOAM BATS

Foam bats are handy for trimming large bowls, shallow bowls, plates, and pots with altered rims that aren't round and level. The foam protects and grips their rims so they won't shift as the bat spins on the wheel head. When trimming on a foam bat, make sure your pot has a good center of gravity; these bats won't work for vertical forms. Also keep the pot securely in place by resting your hand on it as you trim.

Place a bat on top of a piece of ½-inch-thick (1.3 cm) foam. Trace around the bat with a marker; then cut along the traced line. Apply a generous amount of glue to the bat, align the foam disk on top, and press down on it to secure it in place. Let the bat dry for a day before placing it on your wheel head. To make concentric rings on the foam, hold a marker steadily in one position as the wheel rotates the bat. **1**

■ CHUCKS

Chucks are useful for trimming closed forms that can't be balanced upside down, such as a bottle or vase with a small opening (see the Tulipiere project on page 96). They're also handy for working the bottoms of narrow-rimmed pots and for holding them upside down to dry. You may want to make several chucks in a range of different sizes to accommodate different pots. **2**

Center 4 pounds (1.8 kg) of clay on a bat and sink a hole in the middle, all the way to the bat. Next, open the hole, using a claw-like grip with your left hand and resting your right hand on top of the left. Pull the clay toward your body to form a ring of clay. **3** Now pull the ring as you would to create the walls of a cylinder, beginning with a power pull and proceeding with pulls that taper inward in the middle and outward at

the rim. **4** The walls should be 5 to 6 inches (12.7 to 15.2 cm) tall, and about ½ inch (1.3 cm) thick so that they're sturdy.

Use a metal rib to shape the cylinder, giving it a waist area and a flare toward the rim. **5** Cut a channel at the base, release the chuck with a wire, take the bat off the wheel, and leave the chuck in place to dry. Chucks can be used when they're leather hard or after they've been bisque fired.

▋ SLIP

Slip, which at the most basic level is simply a liquid form of clay, is used for slip casting, for adding texture to pots, and as a form of glue for making attachments. To make your own, collect the slurry that accumulates in your bucket of throwing water or the wheel's splash pan. (Even bone-dry scraps of clay can be saturated and used as slip.) Keep the slurry in a small bucket or covered container so it won't dry out.

Thick slip—unlike the colored slip used for dipping and pouring—should be about as thick as yogurt. **6** If it's too thick, just add water; if it's too thin, add slurry. To even out its consistency, blend it with an electric hand blender. When you make this kind of slip from throwing scraps, you may want to sieve the grog out of it first. Place a sieve over a bucket, and work the slip through it with a rubber rib. **7** The finer the mesh size of the sieve you use, the smoother your slip will be. You can use the sieved slip as is or add a colorant (usually sold in powdered form). See page 70 for descriptions of some of the ways that slip can be applied to create design elements and patterns.

■ BISQUE-FIRED STAMPS AND CHOPS

Using stamps to make impressions in moist pottery is a fun and easy way to add texture to your pieces. **8** One way to make your own stamps out of clay is to press a small piece of clay onto an object with an interesting texture. Another is to roll a coil of clay over an item such as a grate, section of mesh, piece of tree bark, button, or shoe sole. **9** You probably have several items around your home that would work well for making good stamps, so keep an eye out for them.

To make a basic stamp, roll out a small coil of clay, 3 inches (7.6 cm) long and ½ to 1 inch (1.3 to 2.5 cm) thick. Tap one end of the coil on a smooth surface to widen it. Smooth that surface with your thumb, and then use a wooden tool to make impressions and patterns in it. **10** Another technique is to let the coil become leather hard and then use carving tools to make detailed marks on it. The stamped design on your pot will be a mirror image of the design or texture that you've pressed or carved into the coil; recessed lines will be raised, initials reversed, and so on.

Chops are personalized stamps that potters use to identify their work. Many potters mark pots with their initials; others use symbols or icons. To make your own chop, start by forming a coil, just as you would for a stamp. Then roll a very thin coil. To create your design, arrange small sections of the thin coil on scored areas of the wide end of the larger coil. Use a needle or a wooden tool to gently work their edges into the chop. **11**

Fired clay stamps and chops are porous and therefore less likely to stick to your pots, so when they're bone dry, bisque fire them. Make a whole bunch of stamps. They'll fit nicely around the pots in the next kiln load.

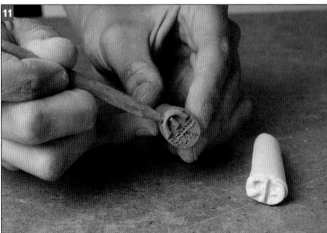

Recipes

Creating your own slips and glazes is a great way to gain an understanding of the materials from which they're made. Many potters gather recipes, experiment with and test them, and eventually establish palettes of their own. When you're ready to invest in the time, space, and materials required to mix slips and glazes from scratch, try some of the recipes provided here. I used them—or ones very similar to them—on the projects in this book. Note the firing temperatures in them (and in all recipes) to make sure that your clay is compatible with the slip or glaze you'd like to use.

You'll need a few special items: a respirator; rubber gloves; a metric scale (either beam or digital); a scoop; three 1-gallon (3.8 L) buckets; a long stick, or a drill and paint-mixing attachment; a rubber rib; and a 40-mesh sieve.

Weigh and mix the dry ingredients outdoors or in a very well ventilated area. And *always* wear a respirator and gloves when you're working with slip and glaze ingredients.

In standard glaze recipes, the amounts of the *base materials* are expressed as percentages of the whole, or as volumes, and usually total 100 percent. (Think of base materials as similar to the ingredients in a plain-vanilla cake recipe.) The amount of the colorant, however, is given as a percentage of the total weight of the dry base ingredients, so you'll weigh it last. One gallon (3.8 L) of glaze usually requires

2,000 grams (2 kg) of dry materials. Always test a new recipe before mixing a large batch! First mix a small test batch (about 200 grams); then glaze and fire a small piece or tile.

Begin by putting on your respirator and gloves. Weigh each of the dry ingredients into a 1-gallon (3.8 L) bucket. Then combine all of the ingredients in a second bucket and mix them together by hand. Add water—about 1 quart (1 L) at a time—and mix the glaze well. The amount of water each glaze requires varies, so add it gradually until the glaze is the consistency of whole milk, or as indicated in the recipe.

Place a sieve over the third bucket, and pour the glaze through it, working any clumps through the sieve with a rubber rib. Sieve the glaze once more, back into the first bucket. Label that bucket clearly with the glaze recipe and firing temperature.

WHITE SLIP, CONE 04–10

Apply to leather-hard clay.

EPK (Edgar Plastic Kaolin)	25.0
Ball clay	20.0
Nepheline syenite	25.0
Silica	30.0
Total	100.0

Green: Add 4% chrome oxide
Blue: Add 7% cobalt carbonate
Dull red: Add 15% red iron oxide
Mix to the consistency of heavy cream.
Apply by brushing or dipping.

CLEAR GLAZE, CONE 04

Apply to bisqueware.

Gerstley borate	55.0
EPK (Edgar Plastic Kaolin)	30.0
Silica	15.0
Total	100.0

HONEY YELLOW GLAZE, CONE 04

Apply to bisqueware.

Gerstley borate	55.0
EPK (Edgar Plastic Kaolin)	30.0
Silica	8.0
Rutile	7.0
Total	100.0

CHUN CELADON, BLUE/TURQUOISE GLAZE, CONE 6

Apply to bisqueware.

F-4 Feldpsar	38.0
Whiting	14.0
Zinc oxide	12.0
Ball clay	6.0
Silica	30.0
Total	100.0

Add:
2% copper carbonate
1% bentonite

TURQUOISE MATTE GLAZE, CONE 6

Apply to bisqueware.

Nepheline syenite	69.0
Strontium carbonate	26.0
Bentonite	3.0
Gerstley borate	2.0
Total	100.0

Add:
4% copper carbonate

CLEAR GLAZE, CONE 6

Apply to bisqueware.

Gerstley borate	20.0
Wollastonite	10.0
Nepheline syenite	30.0
EPK	10.0
Silica	30.0
Total	100.0

Add:
2% bentonite

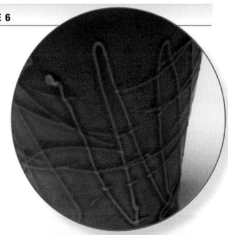

Glossary of Ceramic Terms

Atmosphere. The oxygen-to-fuel proportions within a firing kiln

Banding wheel. A mobile turntable that elevates and rotates pottery for decorative work

Bat. A plaster, Masonite, plastic, or dense fiberboard surface that is attached to the wheel head and on which pottery is made and transported

Bisque ware. Pottery that has undergone an initial low-temperature firing process that renders it porous for glazing

Bone dry. The driest state that clay can reach from exposure to the air

Calipers. A tool used to measure internal and external diameters

Ceramic. Clay that has been fired to a state of chemical conversion

Chuck. A form for supporting inverted pottery for trimming or drying

Clay body. A workable mixture of clays, fluxes, and fillers

Cone, pyrometric. A small, elongated pyramid of ceramic material formulated to measure heat-work inside the kiln

Coning. The preliminary step to throwing, in which clay is formed into a cone shape in order to introduce moisture and compress the clay particles

Earthenware. A clay body; earthenware matures at a low temperature range.

Firing. The heating process that turns clay into a ceramic material, and that fuses glazes to the surface of pottery

Flux. Compounds used to lower the melting point of a glaze and to help it fuse to the clay body

Foot. The base of a pot

Glaze. A liquid mixture of silica, flux, and a stabilizer. Applied to pottery and fired, it decorates and seals the surface.

Greenware. Pottery that is unfired

Grog. Pulverized particles of fired clay, graded in various sizes. Added to a clay body to texturize it, and to decrease shrinkage and warping

Heat-work. Kiln temperature rise per hour

High-fire. A high temperature kiln-firing range, approximately 2280°F to 2383°F (1249°C to 1306°C; cone 8–12)

Inlay. A decorative technique in which a scratched surface design is filled with slip or underglaze

Kiln. A piece of equipment used to fire pottery

Kiln furniture. The stilts and shelves that support pottery in the kiln during firing

Kiln wash. A mixture of refractory materials used to coat and protect kiln furniture

Leather hard. A stage of dryness in which clay is stiff but soft enough to be carved, trimmed, or attached to another piece of clay

Low-fire. A low temperature kiln-firing range, approximately 1087°F to 2106°F (586°C to 1152°C; cone 022–3)

Mid-range. A middle temperature kiln-firing range, approximately 2124°F to 2262°F (1162°C to 1239°C; cone 4–7)

Neutral. A kiln atmosphere in which complete combustion occurs; the balance of oxygen and fuel is perfect and efficient.

Oxidation. A kiln atmosphere in which more oxygen is present than is needed to burn the amount of fuel provided.

Plasticity. The property of moist clay that allows it to be shaped and retain its shape

Porcelain. A white and dense high-fire clay body

Porosity. A quality of clay that has been fired to a low temperature; pores remain open enough for water to seep through.

Pull. The motion of hands as they stretch clay during throwing or forming handles

Pyrometer. A kiln temperature-reading device

Reduction. A kiln atmosphere in which there is more fuel than oxygen; results in incomplete combustion

Rim. The lip or opening of a pot

Sgraffito. A decorative technique in which a layer of slip or underglaze is scratched through to reveal the clay underneath

Shrinkage. The decrease in size of clay as it dries and when it's fired

Silica. A glass former used in clay and glaze formulations

Slip. A liquid form of clay used to make attachments and for decorative effects

Slurry. Water-saturated clay scraps

Stabilizer. Raw clay or minerals used in glazes to prevent excessive melting

Stain. A manufactured color additive for slip, underglaze, and glaze

Stoneware. A dense mid-range or high-fire clay body

Thermal shock. The rapid cooling or heating of ceramic wares; can result in cracking

Thermocouple. A heat-sensitive probe connected to a pyrometer for reading kiln temperatures

Throw. To form pottery using a potter's wheel

Trim. To remove excess clay from pottery

Underglaze. Liquid ceramic pigment applied to greenware or bisqueware for decorative effects

Vitrification. The hardest state to which a clay body can be fired without deformation

Wax resist. A waxy coating that is applied to bisqueware to block glaze absorption

Wedging. Kneading clay to even out its consistency, improve its workability, and remove air

Contributing Artists

Andersen, Stanley Mace
Bakersville, North Carolina
Pages 51, 81, 102

Ash, LeAnne
Lexington, Kentucky
Page 79

Birkhimer, Bradley C.
Manassas, Virginia
Pages 50, 103

Bohnert, Jason
Flagstaff, Arizona
Pages 52, 78

Britt, John
Bakersville, North Carolina
Pages 80, 102

Carpenter, Kyle
Asheville, North Carolina
Pages 52, 81

Carter, Benjamin
Gainesville, Florida
Page 101

Cornish, Scott
New Galilee, Pennsylvania
Page 100

Fielding, Marty
Middlebury, Vermont
Pages 51, 78

Floyd, Becca
Mars Hill, North Carolina
Pages 80, 100

Granatelli, Silvie
Floyd, Virginia
Pages 50, 79, 100

Kelleher, Matt
Penland, North Carolina
Pages 50, 53, 80, 102

Kieffer, Kristen
Baldwinville, Massachusetts
Pages 50, 78, 103

Leitson, Leah
Asheville, North Carolina
Pages 51, 103

Lloyd, Becky
Clyde, North Carolina
Pages 51, 52, 53, 79, 80, 101

Lloyd, Steve
Clyde, North Carolina
Pages 51, 52, 53, 79, 80, 101

Naples, Lisa
Douglastown, Pennsylvania
Page 53

Noble, Brooke
Bloomingdale, New York
Page 52

O'Briant, Kelly
Julian, North Carolina
Pages 78, 100

Rogers, Lindsay
Burnsville, North Carolina
Pages 53, 81

Shankin, Ellen
Floyd, Virginia
Page 102

Sheehan, Joey
Candler, North Carolina
Page 101

Teruyama, Shoko
Penland, North Carolina
Pages 53, 81

Emily Reason
Dotted Teapot, 2007

6 x 9 x 6 inches
(15.2 x 22.9 x 15.2 cm)
Wheel thrown porcelain; assembled, slip trailed; cone 10, reduction fired
Photo by Artist

About the Author

EMILY REASON HAS BEEN WORKING WITH CLAY SINCE SHE PARTICIPATED IN A HIGH-SCHOOL CERAMICS CLASS. Enthralled with clay, she studied ceramics throughout the school year and during summers at the Pittsburgh Center for the Arts. In 2002, she received her BFA degree from West Virginia University, with a concentration in ceramics and a minor in art history.

Subsequently, Emily completed a resident artist's program at Odyssey Center for Ceramic Arts, in Asheville, North Carolina, where she worked in exchange for studio space and access to classes and workshops. Here, she was exposed to methods of working in clay that weren't taught in school, and had the opportunity to gain teaching experience and to exhibit her work. She also participated in the resident artist's program at EnergyXchange, a crafts business incubator in Burnsville, North Carolina, that was established to support artists as they start, manage, and operate their own craft businesses. This experience allowed her to make the transition into her profession as a potter.

Emily's work has been exhibited at the Philadelphia Museum Craft Show; the Smithsonian Craft Show; the annual conference of the National Council on Education for the Ceramic Arts (NCECA); the Society for Contemporary Craft in Pittsburgh, Pennsylvania; Mudfire, in Decatur, Georgia; the Blue Spiral 1 Gallery in Asheville, North Carolina; and the Louisville Visual Arts Association in Louisville, Kentucky. Her work was featured in an article titled "A Reasoned Approach," in the November, 2007 issue of *Ceramics Monthly*, and can be seen at www.emilyreason.com.

She now works as a full-time potter, and teaches classes and workshops in wheel throwing. Emily makes functional pottery, and works primarily with porcelain clay and the potter's wheel. Her studio is in Marshall, North Carolina.

Emily has a deep respect for family, community, friends, nature, travel, and food, all of which motivate, inspire, and nurture her love of pottery.

ACKNOWLEDGMENTS

I WOULD LIKE TO THANK THE PEOPLE WHO HAVE INSPIRED AND SUPPORTED ME THROUGHOUT THE MAKING OF THIS BOOK:

• My parents, **David** and **Peggy Reason**, for their unconditional love and support
• My older brother, **Matthew**, and sister, **Jessica**, whose lives exemplify the fact that with passion and hard work, people truly can live their dreams
• **John Britt**, my good friend and mentor, for his generosity, encouragement, and humor
• **Bob Anderson**, my teacher, for providing my ceramics foundation and instilling in me the values of craftsmanship and commitment
• My friends in the clay community and beyond, who bring me happiness, share their knowledge, and inspire me, and who have helped me in so many ways throughout my career
• I'd also like to thank the Lark Books team that made this book possible: Suzanne Tourtillott, Chris Rich, Linda Kopp, Amanda Carestio, Gavin Young, Kathy Holmes, Carol Morse, and Lynne Harty.

Index